SAVING GRACE

SAVING GRACE

What Patients Teach Their Doctors about Life,
Death, and the Balance in Between

David D. Alfery, MD

RESOURCE *Publications* · Eugene, Oregon

For Joyce, Alli, Janna, and Kim

Let us then approach God's throne of grace with confidence,
so that we may receive mercy and find grace
to help us in our time of need.

HEBREWS 4:16

CONTENTS

AUTHOR'S NOTE

FOR THIRTY-SIX YEARS, I had the greatest job in the world—American medical doctor. Don't let anyone, and especially not any physician, tell you differently. There was no more rewarding profession in the United States than being a physician taking care of patients in the 1980s, 1990s, and the first two decades of the twenty-first century.

I went to LSU Medical School in New Orleans, Louisiana, and then, after a surgical internship at the University of Kentucky in Lexington, Kentucky, I spent another three years at the University of California, San Diego, learning how to become a cardiac anesthesiologist. During those eight years, I was taught about diseases—those that could make you a little sick, those that could make you seriously sick, those that could make you feel sick for the rest of your days, and those that could kill you. With my anesthesia training, I learned how to bring you as close to death as you will ever come to in this life—all in an attempt to forestall your death—and then bring you safely back. The focus was on keeping you alive for as long as possible, often regardless of your prognosis. Even after entering private practice, it took me quite a few years to appreciate that I was learning just as much about living as I was about dying when I worked in my profession.

While my formal education taught me medicine, I attained most of what I came to know about becoming a good doctor and understanding how death influences and shapes our lives—how, in fact, it often teaches us how to live—from my interactions with the patients I was allowed to care for. None of that could ever be experienced without patients entrusting me to work on their behalf. Being trusted, really, with their lives. Remarkably, I was often given that trust within five or ten minutes of meeting them in the holding area of surgery. Accepting that responsibility was the highest honor of my life. The additional benefits that came from being a physician—the financial rewards, the societal status, the intellectual curiosity fulfilled, the satisfaction of a job well done, and all the rest—were far less than the privilege of treating patients in their darkest hours. Above all, I hope that sentiment is borne out in the pages that follow.

In this book, all the stories happened as described. I have tried to reconstruct events as accurately as possible. Conversations are quoted as best as I can remember them, and at the least they reflect the truth of the events that occurred. Except for my wife Joyce and my daughter Alli, I have changed the names of patients and care givers to provide anonymity.

INTRODUCTION

"GODDAMN DRUNKS."

The patient before us, a 19-year-old girl, had been trapped in a burning car after an accident caused by a drunk driver a week and a half earlier. The words were spoken by Dr. John Carter, my second-year surgery resident, a doctor two years ahead of me in training. I was a lowly surgical intern, just one month out of medical school. John issued his curse slowly, as if it might be difficult to understand what his words meant, but I suspect the real reason was because there was so little else to say. He repeated it once, with a grimace, slowly turning his head back and forth. "Goddamn drunks. Gotta get 'em off the roads."

There was no way you could look at the patient and identify her as a 19-year-old female. I knew her age and gender only because I'd seen her chart. We were on rounds in the Burn Intensive Care Unit (ICU) at the Albert Chandler Medical Center at the University of Kentucky, and I was being introduced to the patients I would help care for during the second month of my internship. The girl had recently graduated from high school and appeared to have been slender and delicate, as much as one could tell from the form underneath the dressings. One of the ICU nurses remarked that she had been beautiful, but there were no pictures of her in the Unit. There was only what was left of her. I didn't note her name at the time, but I should have, as patients who have been disfigured this badly should always have a name. After all, that is the one thing you can't take from them after they have lost everything else.

Most of her burns were third degree, and they covered more than 80 percent of her body. You wouldn't know it was 80 percent because she was wrapped head to toe in bandages, with only some monitoring and life-lines such as intravenous (IV) tubing, a urinary catheter, and a breathing tube exiting. The breathing tube had been placed at the time of admission and was a primary reason she had lasted as long as she had.

At the time, 1976, we calculated expected patient mortality by adding the percentage of body surface with third degree burns to the patient's age. The total gave you the percent chance that your patient would die from the injury. You can do the math as well as I can. There would be no saving Grace—I finally learned her name few day later. It was almost certain Grace would not survive no matter what we did, no matter how hard we tried, no matter how hard she fought. Nowadays, we no longer call her burns third degree. The newer name is "full thickness," but they are just as much a killer now as they were then.

So, it was kind of a medical miracle, though not necessarily the good kind, that she was still alive. And you could make no mistake that she was, at least mentally, very much alive. The only visible parts of her were her big brown eyes peering out from the dressings that wrapped around her head. Those eyes would silently follow us around the bed as we moved from one side to the other. We should have been able to see her eyelids as well, but they had been pretty much burned off at the time of the accident. Her pupils were almond saucers in a sea of white, the white of her sclera blending in with the white of the surgical dressings. And everything white except, of course, the blotches of blood that had inevitably seeped through the wrappings. With a breathing tube in place, she made no sound. The only thing audible was the rhythmic whoosh of the ventilator keeping time with the chirping of the electrocardiograph (ECG) monitor. A sickly medicine smell of burn dressings and ointment overpowered the room, an odor of hopelessness.

Twice since admission, Grace had been brought to surgery for skin grafting—taking undamaged skin and transferring it to cover burned areas. But with only 20 percent left available for harvesting, the good skin that would serve as a biological dressing was quickly used up. We would muse about where we might get some more cover for her –a cadaver, an animal? What we did instead was just cut off the dead tissue to the point that we reached live tissue, and you knew you had gotten to that point because the area being worked on would begin to bleed profusely. That particular procedure is called "debridement," but that is just a sanitized medical name for working through the dead parts to get to those still living. When finished, you ended up with, literally, a bloody mess of a patient. A few hours later, back in the ICU, she would gradually regain consciousness, peering out again with glazed eyes that were mercifully dulled by morphine.

Right from the start, I felt a kind of overwhelming helplessness in regard to our efforts, and I knew the other surgical team members did as well. Of course, we did our best to debride the burns, medicate the pain, ventilate the lungs, transfuse the blood loss, and fight the inevitable infections. But we fell miserably short of giving her any kind of physical comfort or reassurance about herself or her future. We couldn't predict other than to know for certain that, in the unlikely event Grace survived, it would be grim. She would remain horribly disfigured—you can't imagine what a burn survivor looks like with her amount of injury—and physically limited by scarring and contractures. Not to mention the psychological impairment of living as a kind of medical freak. Really, it was no life at all if her life continued beyond the Albert Chandler Medical Center Burn Intensive Care Unit. But she was 19 years old, with the same hopes and love of life that we all shared at that age. So, she received our most aggressive medical interventions and, at least for a few weeks, they prolonged her life.

If there were no possibility of a favorable outcome, you might ask, why did we work so hard to save her? What else were we to do? I think we were all in such profound denial of just how horrid the situation was, that we leaned in as closely as we could and focused on the intricacies of her care. We never stood back far enough to see Grace as a whole person whose suffering was almost unbearable to witness, much less endure. Doctors in training back in the 70s (and many still today) learned only how to treat patients, not how to withhold treatment. Giving up was simply not done. Death was the stamp of failure.

Every day on rounds John would mutter the same words, "Goddamn drunks," with the same bitterness, the same futility. Every day entering the ICU, John would have a gloomy frown on his face, looking nowhere, mumbling to no one in particular. Every day we approached Grace's bedside slowly, reluctantly, as if we were one positive pole on a magnet and Grace was the same, with a kind of invisible force keeping us at a distance. And every day, we departed from her bedside as quickly as possible, cringing, having done our best to keep the sinking ship afloat a little longer. Sadly, I don't ever recall meeting Grace's parents until the day she died.

That day we were called to a code—someone's heart had stopped beating—in the Burn Unit. Even before we arrived, we knew who it was. John took over directing the cardiopulmonary resuscitation (CPR) already in progress, but I could tell right away this was not going to be the over-aggressive approach so often seen in that situation. He ordered that a few of the standard drugs be given, going through the motions more than anything else. But when the medications had no noticeable effect he terminated the efforts, and the beautiful, 19-year-old girl was allowed to die. I suspect we all felt a sense of relief that we would not be pushing on her chest and giving resuscitation drugs, not performing hopeless surgeries, giving antibiotics, and making all the other futile and temporizing measures we had at our disposal. Our patient had been a seaworthy young vessel, but the burn had placed a fatal crack in her hull. Since the event, water had been rushing in faster than we had been able to bail it out. At last, the agonizing voyage had ended, the ship sunk, no survivors. Dead at 19.

But how to come to grips with that outcome in a previously healthy and vibrant young patient? More immediately, how to relate Grace's death to her grief-stricken parents? Likely, they had held out hope against hope for several weeks, not fully comprehending what was going on with their daughter, but in their gut comprehending all too well. They had trusted the medical team to do whatever they could for her, whatever they thought best, and now it was over. How do you even begin to tell them? Maybe you start with, "Goddamn drunks?"

John called for her parents to be brought to a "quiet room," to meet there with him, one of the ICU nurses, and me. These rooms are found throughout a hospital, in every hospital, and one is always adjacent to an ICU. Nothing good happens in them. The rooms all look the same, except for maybe a cross and a picture of Jesus in the Catholic and Protestant hospitals. Lighting is muted. They are invariably small, cheerless, non-descript spaces usually consisting of a few chairs, a table and lamp, and perhaps a sofa, where families are brought to learn in private that the worst of their fears has been realized. They are enclosed and private, with a windowless door that shuts securely so there are no outside observers, no distracting noises. As important, the families' responses are not audible or visible for others to witness. I don't recall if a chaplain was with us or not, but I have to think so, as John was the kind of doctor who would not miss including such an important person. Of course, I didn't really know John—Dr. Carter—at the time. He was rail thin, angular, almost chiseled. I suspect that was because, as a surgery resident, there wasn't a whole lot of time to eat. In an earlier life he could have passed for Abe Lincoln's brother, though one who looked older than his stated age. He usually wore a look on his face that was part scowl and part sardonic grin, and he had plenty of occasions for both. On this day he looked like the model in an art class where the assignment was to draw a portrait of Melancholia. I knew he was super smart, with skilled hands, but it wasn't until the meeting with the parents that I truly knew what he was about.

John sat in a chair opposite the parents and moved it towards the couch, close to them. He took the mother's hands in his. He leaned forward and spoke softly, slowly. He looked back and forth into both parents' eyes as he talked, with sad eyes of his own. He told them pretty directly that Grace's heart had stopped, that we had tried to restart it, but that she had passed away. I think he said something religious, something like the Lord has taken her, but I really can't say for sure. What I do remember, and I remember it the way you recall where you were on 9/11 or when the Challenger blew up, was what he told them at the end of the meeting. He said tenderly, "I want you to know that it was a *privilege* to take care of your daughter." And I remember being so taken aback by that statement, by the tribute to the worth and dignity of their child that it expressed. I remember less well the quiet response of the parents and their expressions of gratitude to John and the staff of the Medical Center. John had given the parents a gift they could hold onto after they buried Grace. He had given me a gift as well.

Many individuals, of course, have professions in which they are privileged to interact with others and to profoundly affect their lives. I was fortunate to be one of them. For all good doctors, the kind you want looking after you, there is a transition where you go from thinking that the patient is there for you, to realizing that you are there for the patient. When you understand that it is an honor to be trusted with another person's life, medicine becomes your profession rather than your job, and someone you take care of becomes a unique individual with needs rather than a patient with a number. Only then can you fully embrace the shared humanity that binds physicians to their patients. For me, I think it began on the day I heard Dr. John Carter speak to those parents.

I left the surgery program at the end of my internship year and pursued training to become a cardiothoracic anesthesiologist instead, but I never lost the understanding that there could be nothing more sacred than the well-being of the patients who put their trust in me. I felt the weight of the privilege of taking care of another human being most acutely when death loomed large in the equation. Because I specialized in cardiac anesthesia and spent all but one year of my thirty-six-year career working in tertiary hospitals, those where the sickest patients were cared for, the specter of death seemed to be never far away. Hardly a week went by without an encounter with patients who feared death, or who came close to dying with their surgery. Some presumed, erroneously, there was no chance of dying with their operation, and they still perished. Some died no matter what we did, as if it were pre-ordained. Some died for no good reason other than they needed life-saving treatment and were in the wrong place, at the wrong time. There were miraculous saves in seemingly hopeless situations and jolting losses in those you least expected.

Like many medical students in the United States, I took a modified version of the Hippocratic Oath when I graduated. The original Oath dated back approximately twenty-four centuries, and it is the earliest expression of medical ethics in the Western world. In it, the principles of patient autonomy (patients deciding for themselves the treatment they wish to receive) and confidentiality were first introduced into the practice of medicine. It also, in one widely used version, speaks of life and death:

> Most especially must I tread with care in matters of life and death. If it is given to me to save a life, all thanks. But it may also be within my power to take a life; this awesome responsibility must be faced with great humbleness and awareness of my own frailty. Above all, I must not play at God.[1]

Like most of my classmates, I was overwhelmed with finally becoming a doctor, and I paid little attention to the actual vows we took that day. But it didn't take reciting the Hippocratic Oath to appreciate the authority we were given when we entered our profession; that came almost immediately, when we assumed direct patient care. How to fulfill that responsibility is a learning process that extends over a physician's entire practice life.

The ways I thought about death evolved, as I stumbled through my career, growing little by little, from a mostly abstract condition that I fought against with my skills to one that was a deeply personal bond between those I cared for and me. Likewise, my perception of dying patients progressed from dispassionate detachment to seeing them as fellow human beings in pain.

In the chapters that follow, you will learn a little about my path into anesthesiology and quite a lot about what those working in anesthesia do each day. More importantly, I chronicle what it was like for an anesthesiologist

1. Louis Lasagna, Academic Dean of School of Medicine at Tufts University, 1964.

to deal with death in its many manifestations and presentations over the course of a career In some chapters, death seems deceptively far away, like a gun you are aware of only by the echo of its firing. In others, it makes a direct hit. Just as the patients I describe are unique, my interaction with each tells a distinctive story—the exhilaration one feels when a life is preserved, the terror when a life is on the line, the shock of an unexpected demise, the grace some patients evidence when facing the end of life, the helplessness one suffers when a family member is perilously close to dying, and many more. What unites these chapters is that each explores a component of what makes all of us human.

Chapter 1

RESPECT

ON MY VERY FIRST day of medical school, in my very first class, I flunked my very first test on caring for a patient. That was all the more remarkable because the first patient I met was already dead.

On that first day, in June of 1972, following the first lecture in my Gross Anatomy class at LSU Medical School in New Orleans, I marched into our cadaver lab along with the three classmates with whom I would share a dead body for the next twenty weeks. We went to our assigned stations, denoted by a sticker on a metal case, around which four stools were neatly placed. After we were directed to, we opened the lid, and we leaned over. A sickly aroma wafted up out of the metal container, a cross between a smell of medicine and an industrial cleaner. Our cadaver lay naked. She—ours was a female—looked to be elderly, perhaps seventy years old, maybe more. She was short, probably not much taller than five feet. She must have been rail thin at the time of death, perhaps sick for a prolonged period. Her skin was wrinkled and brown, and a waxy sheen reflected off it from the formaldehyde that had preserved her since her passing. The abdomen was sunken in, lying almost flat against her backbone, with her ribcage jutting out above. The ribs were visible on each side, with the skin indented between each. You could easily count them, like steps on a ladder, starting from the bottom and moving up. Shriveled tan puddles sagging against her torso were all that remained of her breasts. A few whips of grey hair stood sentry above her genitals. Her hands were scrawny, with the fingers thin and curled. At their ends, the fingernails were brown and cracked. Shriveled and misshapen ears lay flat against her skull. Her face seemed like a mask, expressionless. She looked ghoulish, hardly human at all. Her lips

1

were thin, depressed and stretched against gums that bore no teeth. Underneath a few scattered hairs where her eyebrows had once been, her eyes were closed. We dared not look under the lids.

Our instructor made some comments about treating our cadavers with reverence, with honor, but I don't think many were listening. I wasn't. I was transfixed. So, this is what you look like when you're dead and preserved. Wow. Creepy. I can't wait to cut her open and find out what's inside. Pondering only what the body that lay before me could teach me, I failed the test of showing respect.

I wasn't the only one. Along with most of my classmates, we often joked about our cadavers. For some reason, which I have long forgotten, we gave our specimen a nickname, but doing so didn't make her any more human to me.

Like many of the students in Anatomy, I considered my cadaver as simply a tool from which I would learn visible—hence the term "Gross"—human anatomy. As disrespectful as many of us were, in some ways it prepared us for the emotional distancing we would later need when we interacted with live patients. Finding the balance between dispassionate detachment and too much empathy for those we would take care of as doctors would be a life-long struggle for us all.

One thing I found after my first day dissecting was that I could never get the smell of the formaldehyde off my hands. You could wash ten times with a variety of detergents or soaps, and the smell would remain. After a while, I just got used to it.

We spent nearly five months carefully dissecting our cadaver to the deepest places inside, from the most innermost portions of her brain to the cavities of her bones. Every part was teased out with a scalpel and scissors and lay exposed, separated from what surrounded it. Everything was brown, or at least a shade of brown, the color you get when you've been dead a long time and kept in a preservative. Each nerve, each muscle, each artery, each everything was identified, and its relationship to the anatomy around it memorized. During the entire process my cadaver was some *thing* to me, not some *one*. I never stopped to consider what kind of a person she had been, what her life had been like, how she had died, and how she had come to make the precious gift of her body to a selfish student like me. And the thought that she might have been more than a body, that a soul might have somehow dwelled deep within her, never entered my mind. As a first-year medical student, I had a lot to learn besides anatomy.

The first two years of medical school consisted primarily of nonclinical subjects, things like Anatomy, Biochemistry, Pathology, and Histology. Our only contact with patients was in our second year Physical Diagnosis class where we were taught how to examine patients.

Between the second and third year at LSU I had the summer for whatever I wished. I arranged an "externship" at a private hospital in Milwaukee, Wisconsin, each day shadowing a doctor who specialized in internal medicine.

Near the end of summer, I was invited to a party. When I walked in, I saw a girl around my age sitting alone on the couch in the living room. She had straight brown hair parted in the middle that extended all the way down her back until it disappeared between her butt and the sofa cushion. If she put a headband on and stuck a flower in her hair, she could have walked right out of the Woodstock Music Festival held six years earlier. Her face was angelic, dazzling, and her eyes shone brightly as she looked up at me, seeming to sparkle. She smiled, and I was smitten. I thought, she's got to be a model, and she's got to have a boyfriend. Before I had a chance to get nervous, I sat down next to her and introduced myself. She told me her name was Joyce and she was a registered nurse working at a private hospital in Milwaukee. More important, before long I learned she had just broken up with a long-standing boyfriend. *Ungawa!*

It seemed we were immediately attracted to each other, as we ignored the party going on around us. As Joyce told me about herself, there was a simplicity and strength about her that drew me in. Her life had been far tougher than mine, as she had put herself through nursing school, working nights and weekends to do so. She was not dependent on anyone, and I wondered if she was ready for another guy in her life. As I told her about myself, it was obvious she was far less impressed with the fact that I was in medical school than I was. I couldn't keep my eyes off her as we spoke. We spent the entire evening together, and most of the next week and a half, until I went back to New Orleans for my third year of study. When I left, we decided to continue our relationship, even though we would be separated by a thousand miles.

In my third year at LSU Medical School, we dove headfirst into full time patient care, taking required nine-week rotations on Internal Medicine, Pediatrics, Obstetrics and Gynecology, and General Surgery. In the fourth year there were additional mandated subjects, but for several months we were able to take elective courses as well. Students who had already chosen

3

their specialty could take senior rotations at universities where they might like to do their advanced residency training. In fact, even to this day, the best way for a medical student to be chosen to train at a specific institution is to take a senior elective there. This allows the residency program to see just how qualified the student is to be chosen in the spring Match that pairs graduating seniors to the places where they will train.

For others like me, who hadn't been able to decide on a specialty, the elective rotations gave us an opportunity to spend a month immersed in the discipline and help us decide. Three years earlier, Gross Anatomy had introduced me to the heart, an organ that captivated me in its function and complexity. Maybe the brain directed where we were headed, but the heart pulled the train. I was torn between cardiology and surgery, with cardiac surgery a distinct possibility as a final goal.

To help with my decision, and to spend another four weeks with Joyce, I did an elective in Pediatric Cardiology in Milwaukee at The Medical College of Wisconsin. That experience strengthened my interest in the heart, but I moved on to a month of Cardiac Surgery at the University of Oregon in Portland. Within a few days in the Pacific Northwest, I was drawn like a magnet to surgery. Here you could repair the heart, not just diagnose its disease.

The first time I scrubbed in with the cardiac surgery team to do a coronary artery bypass grafting operation, or CABG, as it was becoming known, was a turning point. In this operation the heart needed to be absolutely still in order for the surgeon to sew vein grafts onto the tiny arteries that snaked along its surface. The veins were harvested from the patient's legs, and once they were sewn in place would allow blood to flow from the aorta, the large vessel where oxygenated blood exited the heart, to the arteries beyond the point where they were obstructed. Thus, the blood would "bypass" the areas of narrowing. It was plumbing, but plumbing of the most exquisite kind. When the veins were ready, the patient was placed on a cardiopulmonary bypass machine, or heart-lung machine, or simply called "the pump," in order to isolate the heart while the grafts were being sewn. This second form of "bypass" diverted the blood returning to the heart, sent it over a membrane where it received oxygen and got rid of carbon dioxide (just as the lungs would normally do), and then sent it back to the aorta. In this way the heart and lungs were totally excluded from the circulation while the most demanding part of the operation was performed.

4

In order to "arrest" the heart, or stop it from beating, to give the surgeon a motionless target to work on, a solution with a high concentration of potassium was pumped into the arteries that fed it. In order to cool the heart and lower its oxygen requirements, since it was totally deprived of blood flow while the grafts were being sewn down, an ice-cold saltwater solution was poured over the heart once it had stopped beating

With all the measures taken to avoid injury to the heart, it never really dawned on me that there was a very real chance that a cardiac patient could die during surgery. Looking back, I am astounded by my naiveté, but that ignorance simply reflected the superficial knowledge that characterizes most medical students. Death in the Operating Room was something that occurred in books or in lectures, not in the rooms we were allowed to enter. Accordingly, at no time during my Cardiac Surgery elective did I see a real patient lying on the operating table. There was simply a heart, surrounded by sterile towels, waiting to be repaired.

When I first witnessed the chest being opened, it was otherworldly. After the skin and superficial layers were cut down to the bone, the surgeon took a powered hand saw and inserted its tip up in the neck, in the little bone indentation above the breastbone called the suprasternal notch. Holding the saw in two hands, he powered it on, then pulled vertically down, swiftly cutting through the chest bone from top to bottom in one smooth motion. For those two or three seconds, the high revolutions of the saw were screeching, and fine bone chips flew into the air, a white dust shimmering under the Operating Room lights as they fell back down like snow. Amazing. A large retractor then stretched the chest open, exposing the pericardial sac, the tissue membrane under which the heart lay. I could see the sac moving rhythmically, pushing out slightly with every beat. The surgeon then took a scissors and with a few rapid snips revealed the heart. I stared in wonder. It was magnificent. No drawing of the heart could render what it looked like in person, alive, only a few feet away. The surface was like a map, with various territories and regions delineated by splotches of glistening yellow fat lying like puddles on top of the red muscle. Arteries appeared like branching rivers as they snaked along the surface. It was beating in time, regular, and had been doing so since its early appearance as a one-chambered organ in the fetus at 6 weeks of life, all through its metamorphosis to a 4-chambered pump, until now. How many million times had it beat, I wondered? How could God make such a thing?

My part of the operation was to hold the heart as the grafts were being sewn onto its arteries. After the heart was stopped and the cold solution poured into the chest cavity, the Chief Resident, the senior doctor in training, stretched out my left arm and guided my hand, letting me cup the heart in my palm and fingers. "Just hold your hand still," he commanded. I didn't need to be told. I was frozen, mesmerized, awestruck. I was holding a human heart in my hand. It was cold and firm, just mildly yielding, like a pillow for your back. I squeezed ever so gently, not enough for anyone to notice, and felt a mushy give, as a tenderloin steak might feel with its sides pressed together. The areas of fat on the outside of the heart gently rose up as little hills against the flesh of my fingers, reflecting the uneven surface. The thin upper chamber, the atrium, felt flimsy compared to the thick muscled lower chamber, the ventricle. At my fingertips were the great vessels leading to the lungs and body. I thought again—you are holding a man's heart in your hand. And his life is in the hands of the surgeon. It was glorious. With my arm stretched out and the surgeons leaning over the chest cavity, I couldn't see a thing. I didn't need to. I was hooked.

Well before I finished my rotation in Portland, I made my decision to pursue a career in cardiac surgery, and that meant I first needed to complete an internship and residency in general surgery. I applied to several programs, and I felt fortunate to be selected by my first pick, the General Surgery program at the University of Kentucky.

After I graduated from LSU in June, I took the three-day FLEX Exam for Medical Licensure in Louisiana in order to be able to actually continue on as a doctor. Then I packed up what would fit in my rusted 2-seat MGB sports car and left New Orleans. As I headed north, I thought, "You made it!" Of course, all I'd really done was ascend the first rung on a life-long ladder that all doctors, whether in training or beyond, must climb. Still, I was pretty happy. As I drove, I thought about the last four years. Most of the time had been spent either studying general subjects, like our cadaver in Gross Anatomy, or centered on a system of the body, such as the heart and blood vessels of the cardiovascular system. With relatively few interactions involving patients seen as a whole, the empathy doctors must have for their patients was barely budding. I was callous and naïve, totally ignorant of the enormity of emotions I would experience from a life spent caring for others.

As I drove north, I also thought of the many individuals who had helped me during the past four years—professors, residents, interns—who

I had never even bothered to thank. I thought back to a few of the sick people I had encountered, as well. Like the cadaver in my Anatomy class, I had viewed them more in terms of what they could give me rather than how I could assist with their care. Just as I did my teachers, I realized I owed my gratitude to the patients I had interacted with. Especially the one who was dead when I met her. I vowed to do better.

Chapter 2

DIGNITY

THREE AND A HALF weeks later, I stood at the Operating Room table and stared down at the infant. There was no doubt that she was dead. Dr. Estes had said to turn the pump off, and that was that. Six hours earlier she had been alive after a difficult first year of life, but still, fully alive. And now she lay lifeless before me. They didn't prepare you for that in medical school. Nothing prepared you for that.

Three weeks earlier, when I arrived in Lexington, Kentucky, I'd found a small apartment near the Medical Center. It didn't have much more than a bed and a table, but I wouldn't be there for anything other than sleeping on the nights I wasn't on call. Joyce had moved to Lexington, as well, as our relationship grew more serious, and she had found a job teaching nursing. As we got settled in the small Southern city, my apprehension about the next step grew.

As a medical student, I had taken call with the surgery interns at LSU. They worked at Charity Hospital, one of the oldest and largest hospitals in the United States. It was fast paced, with plenty of critically ill patients to attend to. At the time, I didn't really appreciate how difficult the interns' job was. Now, suddenly, I did.

On the day before our first year of training began, the Surgery Department gave a party for the new interns and for the residents who were advancing onto the next year of training. I met quite a few of my fellow interns, and all the guys—everyone was a male in the program—seemed brimming with confidence. I wondered, what did they have to give them the kind of assurance that I lacked? Looking back, I suspect we were all scared to death.

It was almost a relief when I began the training the next day because, suddenly, my time was so occupied with medicine I hardly had a moment to be frightened. The internship itself was the first year of a four-year track in General Surgery, with the expectation that I would continue on for another two in the Cardiothoracic Surgery program there. The year consisted of twelve-monthly rotations through the various disciplines that surgery encompassed. For my first month of duty, I was assigned to the Cardiac Surgery service.

As a newly minted intern, I was thrilled the first time a nurse called me "doctor." The luster of that wore off pretty quickly, though, because I was also the first person the nurses called for problems with their patients. There were plenty of other firsts for me that month. The first time I admitted a patient after making the correct diagnosis, the first time I performed an actual operation (tracheostomy) and then dictated what I had done in the Operating Room (OR), the first time I placed a breathing tube into a patient. It was also the first time I made a mistake that could have cost a patient their life.

One evening, ten days into the month, I was on overnight call. I was already used to being tired all the time, as we took call every third night, and on those nights, we were lucky if we got even a few hours of sleep. More often than not our heads never hit the pillow. Each day began at 5:45 am and often stretched to 8 pm, so even on the nights we got home, we rarely got enough rest.

I had been down for maybe twenty or thirty minutes when my pager jolted me awake. It was 3:00 am, and I was needed in one of the adult ICUs to see a patient who had surgery earlier that day. I shook the sleep from my head and trudged to the location to find the patient with a blood gas analysis that showed an abnormally low oxygen concentration. I turned up the level of oxygen he was receiving from the ventilator (the machine that gives breaths to a patient who has a breathing tube) from 40 to 50 percent and ordered a STAT portable chest X-ray (STAT meaning it should be done immediately). While I waited for the radiology technician to arrive, I listened to the patient's chest, but I couldn't really hear any abnormality over the noise of the suction catheters draining blood from the middle of his chest. Once the X-ray was taken, I followed the tech down to the Radiology Department, still half asleep. The film slid out of the developer within five minutes, and I wearily snapped it up on an illuminated viewing box. There was a lot that was abnormal to begin with, as one could see pacing wires attached to the heart, other wires holding the breastbone together, and plastic tubes in the mid-chest to drain blood. A separate plastic endotracheal tube (ETT), or breathing tube, was in his airway, and there were multiple metallic dots from his ECG leads on his chest. With all that going on, I somehow missed the large pneumothorax, or collapsed lung, that was present on the left side.

I returned to the ICU and noted the blood gas that was drawn with his increased oxygen concentration was only marginally improved. I increased his concentration to 60 percent and returned to bed.

When the surgical team assembled at 5:45 am, I had slept for less than two hours, but I was grateful for even that. The first thing we always did was review our patients' chest X-rays. The first film up was my patient from 3 am.

One of the second-year residents immediately remarked, "Well, that's a pretty big pneumo. Did he get a chest tube?" The tube, had it been inserted, would have allowed his lung to immediately expand and alleviated his low oxygen level.

I blinked repeatedly, as if to help me focus on the X-ray. I was mortified to see the obvious abnormality I had missed. I had even taken a month-long rotation on Radiology as a senior medical student, so I had no excuse. Had I been confused with all the artifact on the film? Had I been too tired to really focus on the lung fields? I stammered, lamely, "I, I don't know how I missed that. I can't explain it. It's just so obvious."

Gratefully, I wasn't chastised for my error, and we moved along to the other films. I suspect the Chief Resident figured my public humiliation had been enough punishment. A senior resident was dispatched to place the chest tube, and no harm came to the patient. But my miss was a potentially fatal mistake, as a pneumothorax under the tension caused by the ventilator could cause circulatory collapse along with a precipitous drop in the oxygen level. Had the patient died, it would have been my mistake alone that had caused it. I got lucky that night, and my patient did, as well.

From that moment on, I viewed my position with a heightened urgency, a greater seriousness. Good grief, I wondered, is it that easy to kill a patient? I vowed to never again miss a pneumothorax, and I never did. But the incident revealed a dirty little secret of medicine: mistakes are commonly made, and they are most commonly made by those early in their training. Thus, there is an old saying in medicine that rings true to this day: good judgment comes from experience, but unfortunately, that experience is often the result of bad judgment. My error also reflects a notion that most physicians believe about getting care in a teaching hospital—it is best to avoid it in the summer, when those taking care of you are new in their positions.

That first month of my internship was also the first time I witnessed a death in the OR. It came early, only a few days after that missed pneumothorax.

Depending on their subspecialty, there are many seasoned surgeons who have never experienced a patient dying in the OR. It is typical to go through an entire career in urology or ophthalmology or plastic surgery and never face an intra-operative fatality. Not so with cardiac surgery. From the acuity and severity of the illnesses they treat, every cardiac surgeon meets death in the OR from time to time.

While a death during surgery is disturbing to witness; it can be devastating to cause it. For those intimately involved in the care of the patient, there is a wave of emotions that sweeps over you. Some occur immediately, others take time. Shock, disbelief, anger, an overwhelming sense of failure. Did I cause or contribute to this death? What if I had done this, or that, might the outcome have been different? Some doctors never recover. How physicians deal with an intra-operative death was not generally covered in medical schools when I attended, or at least not in mine. I would be taught much about this subject from Dr. Kenneth Holcomb, Chief Resident in cardiac surgery at the University of Kentucky. Most importantly, he would teach me about dignity.

Two weeks into my internship, heart surgery was scheduled on a little girl around twelve months old. She had been born with a major cardiac abnormality that had caused some poorly oxygenated blood returning from her body—blood that was bluish in color—to bypass the lungs and go directly back out to her body's systemic circulation, and thus she carried the common name of a "blue baby." A palliative operation done shortly after birth had allowed her to survive the first year of life, but a chance at any kind of longevity demanded that a far more extensive surgery be done. The operation would be complicated and hazardous. The hand of the patient's family was forced to a certain extent—take a chance with surgery or know she would die young. They accepted the risk and chose the definitive repair.

On the morning of surgery, the anesthesiologist carried the little girl wrapped in his arms into an uncomfortably warm Operating Room. One of the risks of surgery and anesthesia in an infant was a rapid drop in temperature early in the case. We would all sweat under our surgical gowns, for the baby's sake.

Like most children with cyanotic congenital heart disease, she was thin and frail. Fragile, as if she might easily break if mishandled. Everything about her seemed small for her age except her eyes. They were alert and inquisitive, bright, almost twinkling, looking around her. She looked angelic, pure and innocent. She did not cry. Her wispy blonde hair contrasted with the blue in her lips.

As the anesthesia personnel busied themselves with preparing the patient, I went to the scrub sink with Dr. Holcomb. As Chief Resident, he was in the last of six punishing years of postgraduate training. He was around five feet nine inches tall and weighed easily over 200 pounds, a kind of human fire hydrant. He looked Italian, dark complexion with wavy black hair. I envisioned him as a kind of Sylvester Stallone in Rocky, just carrying a little more weight, but with the same kind of swagger and East Coast accent. He was nicknamed The Honey Bear, but no one knew exactly where that came from. Honey Bear Holcomb. I had seen him react to what he had perceived as laziness in one of my fellow interns, so I knew where the bear part originated. I would soon see his soft side, as well.

The Chairman of the Department of Cardiothoracic Surgery and Dr. Holcomb's boss, Dr. Jonathan Estes, soon joined us at the scrub sink. Dr. Estes was tall, maybe six feet three, late-forties, and had managed to keep a pretty athletic build and youthful appearance despite spending the great majority of his time in clinic or standing still at an operating table. His features were angular, with a sharply defined nose and jutting jaw, and his piercing blue eyes looking through wire rimmed glasses seemed to shine on you like the bright lights of an automobile. His hair, while mainly brown, had a few wisps of gray, perhaps from the pressure of his position. Dr. Estes had been trained in pediatric cardiac surgery as well as adult hearts, which made him a kind of cardiac surgery super specialist. Given the skill and experience required to successfully operate on complex pediatric heart disease, Dr. Estes would perform the repair with Dr. Holcomb assisting. As a new surgical intern, I wouldn't have any significant responsibilities during the operation. My job was to simply observe and then assist Dr. Holcomb in closing the chest when the repair was completed.

Neither Dr. Holcomb nor Dr. Estes spoke about the operation as they stood together at the sink. They seemed to have confidence that surgery would be successful, bantering back and forth while washing their hands.

The operation began uneventfully, or at least it seemed that way. I had scrubbed in on a few pediatric heart cases in Portland, and I was captivated each time a small chest was opened to expose the heart, as if I had never seen it before. It was like opening a little jewel box with a glistening, contracting timepiece inside. How could it beat so rhythmically, so constantly, and be so perfect? Except in this case, it wasn't. I could see some of the altered anatomy. An artificial conduit—a thin tube made of Dacron that would carry blood—had been attached to the pulmonary artery, the large vessel that ran from the right side of the heart to the lungs. Where they joined together, tiny blue sutures evenly spaced apart circled from one side to the other, with even tinier little ends where they had been cut off from the tiny knots below them, sprouting up like tiny double blue hairs. The conduit allowed more blood to flow to the lungs and receive oxygen, but with the growth of the little girl over the past year, the repair would no longer prove sufficient. Surgery would entail removing the Dacron graft, opening up the heart, and repairing the defects she had been born with.

As Drs. Estes and Holcomb started work, there was the usual conversation about superficial things, like how the University of Kentucky football team might do that year. The casual talk ceased when the small tubes were placed in the vessels that would be used to put the patient on bypass. Just as in adult cardiac bypass surgery, the heart lung bypass machine cooled the blood in order to reduce the metabolic needs of the child's organs, and while the repair was made, the heartbeat was brought to a standstill.

During those most critical stages of the procedure, the only conversation was an occasional quiet exchange between Drs. Estes and Holcomb.

Aside from removing the previously placed conduit, the operation involved closing a hole that was present between the lower muscular chambers of the heart (called a ventricular septal defect, or VSD) with a patch made of Dacron, trimming a muscular ridge that obstructed blood flow from the right ventricle to the lungs, and opening up the heart valve directly beyond the ridge. With such a small patient, surgery was delicate and exacting. Dr. Estes' hands were large, even large for a man his size, and they dwarfed the little heart as he placed his instruments inside it. Between the two surgeons leaning over the wound, their hands hovering above it, and the small heart they were working inside of, I really couldn't see a thing.

After Dr. Estes had finished correcting the cardiac abnormalities, conversation resumed on meaningless topics while the little girl was rewarmed and the heart began beating again. When it started up, all on its own, it seemed like one of life's impenetrable miracles. How did it know to do that, I asked myself?

When the little girl reached a normal body temperature, her heart would be "rested" for a short time in order to help it recover from having been stopped and deprived of oxygen. That meant there would be an additional interval when the bypass machine would continue to oxygenate and circulate her blood. Since the blood was not yet returning to her heart, the heart didn't have to work at pumping out blood during that time—it could "rest." As we waited, the anesthesiologist began an infusion of a medication to speed up the heart rate while Dr. Holcomb attached pacemaker wires to the surface of the organ. Then he straightened up and stood back. Dr. Estes did as well. They looked like craftsmen, admiring their work. I leaned forward now to get a better view. I could see the heart beating with a steady rhythm, first the upper chamber followed by the lower chamber, just as it should. The muscular right ventricle, the one you could best see, seemed to contract inwards smoothly, reducing in size symmetrically as it should. With the right ventricle seeming to move inwards with vigor as it contracted, it looked strong to me.

Finally, Dr. Estes was satisfied that the heart had recovered sufficiently. He began the process of separating from cardiopulmonary bypass slowly, cautiously, just to make sure everything proceeded smoothly. He did this by allowing a small portion of blood that was going through the bypass machine to flow back to the heart. The blood returning to the heart flowed from the right atrium to the right ventricle, was pushed out to the lungs by the right ventricle contracting, received oxygen in the lungs, returned to the left atrium, and then was finally pushed out to the body by the contraction of the left ventricle. You could judge the ability of the heart to resume this normal flow simply by looking at the right ventricular muscle squeezing inwards, ascertaining that it moved normally. What you did not want to see was the muscle gradually increasing in size, like a balloon slowly inflating. That would mean it was not able to pump blood adequately. The heart looked to be keeping its shape, so Dr. Estes allowed a little more blood to return, with less circulated by the pump. When he had reached the point where three fourths of the blood was being pumped naturally, Dr. Estes was satisfied the little girl's heart could function fully on its own, and he finally said, "Come off." The pump stopped circulating, and all the blood returned to the heart. She was on her own.

The surgeons' eyes focused on the tiny organ. With both of them leaning over the chest cavity, my view was blocked, but I could see the arterial trace on the anesthesia monitor. It should look like a steep mountain with each heartbeat, indicating a vigorous ejection of blood with each contraction, but it barely registered as tiny hills moving across the screen. Dr. Estes mumbled something indistinct, and the anesthesia resident responded in agreement. Within a few minutes the hills had almost flattened, and Dr. Estes commanded sharply, "Back on." He sounded irritated. The pump resumed circulating all the blood. I didn't know what the problem was. Perhaps the infant's heart was not pumping adequately, or maybe there was bleeding which needed to be addressed?

No one spoke.

Dr. Estes called for some suture and went to work. Dr. Holcomb remained silent, assisting. After ten or fifteen minutes, Dr. Estes again eased the patient off of bypass, but this time he put her back on almost immediately. Whatever was going on hadn't been fixed. The room remained silent, except for the chirp of the heartbeat from the cardiac monitor and a soft "whirring" sound as the bypass machine circulated the blood. Occasionally a suction catheter made a gurgling sound as it drew blood out of the surgical field. There was some kind of brief conversation between Dr. Estes and the anesthesia resident and attending anesthesiologist, who then added and adjusted medications.

A third attempt was made to come off, but this time we never even made it past partial bypass. Dr. Estes cursed softly and said something that was inaudible to everyone but Dr. Holcomb, who nodded. I didn't know exactly what was going on, but I understood the possible consequences. If you couldn't come off bypass, you died, so every possible attempt would be made to get her off. I couldn't see what Drs. Estes and Holcomb were doing as they resumed working, their bodies once again hovering over the tiny chest cavity. Even so, I felt the dread in the room rise like water coming up all around, rising as if it would drown us all.

Several more attempts were made to come off, each one less successful then the last. Finally, the surgeons stood back, helpless. I leaned in again and looked down. What had been a beautifully rhythmically contracting organ at the start of the case was almost unrecognizable. The heart was purplish and bruised, angry, discolored by areas of hemorrhage on the surface. It was distended like a small balloon, barely moving inwards with each attempted contraction. I didn't know it at the time, but this was the look of a dying heart.

I can't say how many more attempts were made to come off bypass, though it went on for what seemed like more than an hour. Finally, Dr. Estes stood erect, stepped back, and softly said, "We're done. Turn the pump off." Battle lost, full surrender, total defeat. He stripped off his surgical gloves and gown and quietly thanked everyone in the room. He turned around slowly, as if hesitant to leave. His face was drawn and weary. His head hung low, as though he needed to look at the floor to find his way. He paused for a moment, took one big breath, and then wordlessly shuffled out of the room.

No one spoke.

The individuals still in the room looked at each other—the pump tech (also called "perfusionist") running the heart-lung machine, Dr. Holcomb, the anesthesia personnel, the nurses, the OR techs, me. The only sounds were a steady beep, beep, beep of the dying heart's electrical activity and the whirl of the pump. The pump tech leaned over and flipped a switch. The whirl stopped. I wondered if he had waited for Dr. Estes to leave the room, to spare him from the finality of his action. The anesthesia attending turned off the pacemaker, but the beeps remained, only much slower. Over the next couple of minutes, they drew slower still, as if taking an agonizing last few futile electrical gasps, the last few twitches of life. Finally, mercifully, silence.

There remained work to be done.

The cannulas to the heart lung machine had to be taken out, the pacemaker wires removed, and the chest cavity sewn up. I moved to where Dr. Estes had stood. Dr. Holcomb did his work silently, bent over, robotically focused on each step. As he tied down each suture, he moved his hands slightly away for me to cut it. I did so without speaking. When he got to the last layer to be closed, the skin incision, I was struck by the care he took. He used a subcuticular stitch, one that was placed just under the skin edges and couldn't be seen. This was the stitch one used for the best possible cosmetic results. Each time he drove the needle through he brought the edges together, precisely, perfectly. At the time, I had no idea why he would demand such a meticulous closure. I wish I had been mature enough to understand while I witnessed it.

While the skin was being closed, you could almost pretend that the infant was still alive. But once the drapes were pulled back and her body was fully exposed, there was no denying what had happened. It was awful.

The struggle, the futility, the defeat. And in one so young. I looked down at the little girl and tried to look away. I couldn't. I was uncomfortably drawn to stare at her, to take it all in. Maybe it was to observe the end of where we had traveled over the past six or seven hours. Maybe it was like leaning over to see what was at the side of the road, to see just how bad the accident had been. Whatever it was, I was gripped.

It was as though the axis of the OR had been turned upside down. There was an almost total transformation from the inquisitive little girl that had been carried into the OR, to what now looked like a poorly made, disheveled doll. Her color had darkened to a waxy grey, with dusky blotches of bruising on the surface. After the tape holding her eyes closed had been removed, they were open, pupils widely dilated, staring vacantly. Don't believe anyone who tells you a baby that has just died looks asleep. She looked profoundly unnatural. I could hardly breathe.

With the skin closure completed, Dr. Holcomb began to carefully wash her skin, removing blood and then dabbing it dry. He could have left the OR far earlier, and in fact he could have left the skin closure to me, but he stayed. The anesthesia personnel removed the intravenous lines, the breathing tube, and temperature probes from the esophagus and rectum. The nurses placed trash that was strewn about the room into collection bags. The room felt funereal.

Still, no one spoke.

Dr. Holcomb applied a surgical dressing, lining it up precisely over the incision. He trimmed the lower end so it would fit perfectly. He applied surgical tape on both sides, exactly in line with the dressing. He gently pressed the gummed surfaces down onto the child's bruised chest.

One of the male attendants, likely an orderly, broke the silence and whispered to the room, "Shhh! Don't wake the baby."

Dr. Holcomb froze. He looked up quickly, eyes locked on the speaker. His mask was off, and his face was beet red. He paused for a moment, as if trying think of what to say. The veins on his neck bulged out like ropes. And then he exploded. "What did you say? What did you say? Get the *fuck* out of my Operating Room!" There were tears in his eyes, maybe from anger, maybe from loss. It looked like he wanted to say something more, but no words came out. His breathing was heaving, as if he was trying to catch his breath. The individual who had made the remark slunk out of the room quickly, but with a smirk on his face, not looking back. No one else in the room said a word.

Once the dressing was on, Dr. Holcomb straightened the infant's arms at her side and pulled a clean sheet up neatly to her neck, as if to keep her warm. With his index and long fingers he pulled her upper eyelids closed. He took a step back and paused for a moment while he surveyed the small body, dwarfed by the long operating table. He took a breath, held it briefly, and then let out an audible sigh. Shaking his head slightly side to side, he turned and moved slowly to a counter at the side of the room and picked up the patient chart. He moved again, almost reluctantly, to a stool in the corner. He eased himself onto it and pulled his legs up with his heels on a lower rung. He leaned forward. The chart rested on his knees. He opened it as though to write a summary of what had transpired, but he never even looked down. He just stared out into the room, seemingly lost in thought. Maybe he was thinking about all that had happened. Maybe thinking about tomorrow. Maybe just trying hard not to think at all.

Chapter 3

PARALYSIS

THE DEATH OF THAT little girl hit me hard. Until then, any deaths I'd encountered were at one remove: as a medical student finding an empty bed on morning rounds because the patient had expired overnight, witnessing from a distance a failed gunshot resuscitation in the Emergency Room.

The little girl's death was the slap on the face I needed. Over the next few days, like the sun slowly rising over the horizon, it dawned on me why Dr. Holcomb had been so meticulous with the closure, so thorough cleaning the blood off of her, so precise in aligning the dressing. I thought back to how I'd been four years prior, when I was a first-year student in Gross Anatomy: my, how I had failed. And failed repeatedly as a student, in ways both large and small. All patients who perish need to be treated with dignity. And shouldn't that commitment translate into a priority when you treat live patients? I was learning that if you didn't understand that you had no business becoming a doctor.

The passing of that infant also caused me to question my own existence, in ways I never before had. I had grown up in a family totally devoid of religion, where discussions about the meaning of life had never taken place. Now I wondered, were we all just a flame that burned brightly and then flickered out? If "here today and gone tomorrow" summed up the human condition, why bother to take the journey? I didn't know it, but those disquieting questions were the first sparks of a religious faith that would gradually come into my life.

For the second month of my internship, I was assigned to Grey Surgery, one of two general surgical services at the University of Kentucky. By that time, I had gained some confidence when taking call, because I

19

was rarely paged for anything more serious than Mrs. Baker had not had a bowel movement in three days or the nurses couldn't get an IV into Mr. Rodriguez. Even with more serious medical questions, I'd always had time to look up the answer if necessary. Still, I'd heard about some critical situations that a few of the other interns had faced, and I wondered how I would have measured up.

One evening around 6 pm, my pager went off. First, a high-pitched, rapid-fire beep, beep, beep, beep, beep, and then, "Call 2200 STAT."

I had never been called STAT before—a true emergency—so my heart rate jumped as I scrambled to the nearest phone

I jammed in the number, and the answer was immediate.

"B ward, General Surgery."

"Yeah, Hi. This is Dr. Alfery. I'm the intern on call for . . . " The voice cut me off. "They need you STAT in 216."

"Got it. Coming."

I tossed the phone back in its cradle, already running. I was at the far end of a ward on another wing of the hospital, on the fifth floor. I sprinted down the corridor to reach the main staircase, jerked open the stairwell door, and then descended, jumping two steps at time, steadying myself with the handrail. After three flights, I slammed the door open and ran past the nurses' station, towards the end of the hall and Room 216. Any seriously ill patient would be in the ICU. How could they possibly need me STAT?

Out of breath, I stormed into the poorly lit room, where an elderly male patient was leaning forward, his butt on the mattress, fighting to try to stand up. A diminutive nurse, maybe five feet tall, stood with her back to me, struggling to control him. Her hands gripped his shoulders as she tried to hold the man down. "Calm down Mr. Cooley. Please lean back and just take a deep breath." She must have heard me come in, as she looked back at me over her shoulder; she looked scared.

The man looked wretched and desperate, as he flailed his arms back and forth. His head swiveled right, then left, then right again, as if shaking his head "no." His eyes darted wildly, not settling on anything, and his un-shaven face was drenched in sweat. He struggled against the nurse, gasping, "I can't breathe. Can't breathe."

Only the top bulb of the double light at the head of the bed was on, but I could see he was deeply blue in color, an indication that he was getting far less oxygen into his blood stream than he needed. His breathing was fast, maybe fifty times a minute. We usually picked thirty-five as the cut-off for respiratory failure, the point where a patient might need a breathing tube and a ventilator. The nasal prongs that should have been giving him additional oxygen were pulled down around his neck, the other end dangling limply by his side.

The nurse leaned forward to push him back, pleading, "Please Mr. Cooley. Just breathe. Just try to breathe."

The patient fought and straightened himself. "Can't breathe. Can't breathe."

I hustled forward and grabbed the patient's shoulders and tried to push him back onto his bed, which only made him fight harder. Together, the nurse and I got him tilting back onto his pillows, leaning at around forty-five degrees, but he continued to struggle. With his right arm he gripped my left forearm, trying to pull himself upright. I pushed him back again, thinking, man, he was strong for a guy who looked near eighty. I echoed the nurse's instructions. "Calm down, Mr. Cooley, just breathe. We're going to take care of you."

My mind was racing like a slot machine with all the wheels spinning. All the diagnoses I had learned in school were a jumbled mix in my mind. All the things I might do for the patient were spinning as well, none in focus. All I could think of was to re-apply his oxygen. While his right hand still gripped me, I pulled his prongs up to his nose and cinched the plastic tight from the back of his head. I leaned over and inserted the other end into the oxygen regulator on the wall next to the head of the bed. I cranked the flow meter to 10 liters/minute, as high as it would go.

The nurse looked pretty much like me, a new graduate, innocent and confused. She couldn't have been much more than a hundred pounds—no match for Mr. Cooley. He tried to straighten up again, and together we tried to wrestle him back. She glanced back up into my eyes momentarily and gave a quick report: "This is Mr. Cooley. He's 2 days out from a colon resection and I found him like this. His blood pressure is 80/40 and his pulse is 130."

"Can't breathe. Can't breathe," he gasped again, thrashing violently. Finally, he managed to sit forward enough that the oxygen hose stretched taught from the flow meter at the wall and snapped off.

I pushed him back again and tried to hold him down, but he was slippery with sweat. Now what? Physical examination? Guess at a diagnosis? Initiate some kind of treatment? I yanked my stethoscope out of the right front pocket and tried to get the earpieces into my ears with one hand, pushing Mr. Cooley back with the other. As soon as I got the stethoscope on his chest, he batted it away. I'm not even sure what I would have been listening for. I was really just trying to buy a few seconds, still trying to try to figure out what to do. Above all, I needed to determine just how serious the situation was. I knew he was sick, but how sick? With a blood pressure of 80/40 he couldn't be all *that* sick. But then again, that was pretty low. The heart rate at 130 was awfully high, but patients can tolerate a really fast heart rate. I knew he might need a significant therapeutic intervention other than oxygen, maybe even that breathing tube, but how to know for certain? And how quickly would he need it? Surely, I had some time to work with here, didn't I? He was still breathing, after all. He still had a blood pressure. Would some laboratory blood work assist in making a diagnosis, give me some direction? Should I order a STAT blood gas to see how low his oxygen level was? Should I turn up his intravenous fluid infusion, which might help the blood pressure? My mind continued to spin. The nurse would look at me with eyes wide open, as if to say, "What do we do, doctor?"

Paralyzed, I did nothing.

After perhaps ninety seconds spent struggling with the patient, it suddenly occurred to me I was in over my head. Dr. John Carter was the second-year resident on call with me. I looked at the nurse and half shouted, "Call Dr. Carter STAT." The nurse spun around and fled the room.

I continued to fight with Mr. Cooley, reaching again and applying his oxygen, but he grabbed the tubing and plucked it off like it was a clothesline, ripping the plastic prongs all the way off his head. I leaned in and wrapped my arms around his chest and tried to hold him still.

Within 90 seconds Dr. Carter burst through the door, striding toward us. His eyes locked on Mr. Cooley, and he growled to the nurse following him, "Call a code." She fled.

"Call a code" is universal medical language used in every hospital to summon a special emergency team to treat a patient whose heart has stopped beating or who has stopped breathing, or who is in imminent danger of doing so. The code teams are always available, on call, always specifically designated within a hospital, ready to drop whatever they're doing and respond. The team includes members from each of the disciplines that might be required in a patient crisis: a physician to direct the care, a pharmacist to draw up drugs, a respiratory therapist or anesthetist to manage the breathing, a small army of nurses to pump on a patient's chest if need be, administer drugs, set up IV infusions, and do whatever else might be needed. There is even a designated nurse whose sole responsibility is to record everything being done, along with the exact time it is done.

Within a couple of minutes, the various team members stampeded into the room, converging on the patient and backing me to the wall. Dr. Carter's voice was firm and steady as he "ran the code" (directed the care). Cardiac leads were attached, an additional intravenous catheter was threaded into a vein, a breathing tube was placed into the windpipe, or trachea, and medications were given to elevate the blood pressure. Within ten minutes, before my heart had a chance to slow down, Mr. Cooley was whisked out of the room and rushed to the ICU. I don't know if he lived through his hospitalization or not, but I do know that Dr. Carter and the code team gave him his best chance.

The whole experience left me shaken. I couldn't help wondering if I had delayed much longer than I did, would Mr. Cooley even have survived the code? How close had I been to simply allowing his death?

The first lesson I learned from Mr. Cooley is to accept immediately that when a patient appears in acute distress, they really are as sick as they appear. For doctors in training, there is a natural response to try to deny reality and think, "surely it can't be that bad." Many patients have perished simply because a physician couldn't accept the evidence directly in front of them.

Why might a doctor fail to appreciate the gravity of a critical situation? Of course, the easy answer is denial. A more nuanced explanation factors in confirmation bias, a type of cognitive tilting of the mind that involves favoring information that conforms to ones previously held beliefs or biases. In short, we interpret information that fits our wishes or first impression. If a doctor (me) is called to a crisis and wants to believe that a patient (Mr. Cooley) is not in great distress, he will discount the fact that the patient is fighting his nurse and gasping for breath and over-emphasize the fact that he is still breathing and has a blood pressure. To avoid this trap, doctors must make the mental effort to accept the worst scenario first and discard it only if they definitively prove to themselves that it's not true.

The second lesson I learned is to act decisively. If a doctor doesn't know what to do, he or she must immediately call for someone who does. Many patients have died because their physician was paralyzed with indecision.

Physicians who regularly attend to critically ill patients—cardiologists, pulmonologists, anesthesiologists, emergency room physicians, among others—have these lessons ingrained into their core during training. These are the alpha dogs of medicine. Many other doctors—internists and psychiatrists, for example—often go into specialties that do not require rapid evaluation and decision making simply because they found the pressure of acute critical care so stressful.

One other thing the incident with Mr. Cooley taught me was that a patient didn't actually have to be in full cardiac or respiratory arrest to require a code. If you needed intensive help, and a lot of it, you shouldn't hesitate to call for it. That was the kind of lessen you could never get in a textbook. You have to experience it before it sinks in.

One thing my interaction with Mr. Cooley did *not* teach me was how to know when to cease efforts at resuscitation, to terminate a code. In time, I would learn that sometimes those decisions would be relatively easy, as they were with Grace, our 19-year-old burn patient. When there's no prospect the patient can return to a relatively healthy life, when successful restoration of breathing and a heartbeat mean further misery, the person in charge of the code can quit without remorse. But when a full life can be looked forward to, especially in a younger patient, the burden that comes with ending a code, or "calling it" (ironically, the same the term we use for initiating our efforts), can be soul crushing. It still remained to be seen if I was up to that responsibility.

Chapter 4

TRUST

AS MY RESPONSIBILITIES AS an intern increased, I was struck by how easily dignity could be lost in a hospital. The pace of my work was frenetic, but whenever I had a moment to look around me, I could see countless ways that patients could be made to feel vulnerable or unimportant. In the hub-bub of a hospital setting, it is easy to forget that it is fellow human beings, rather than organ systems or "cases," that we're dealing with. From the lack of privacy that flimsy hospital gowns provide, to conversations among col-leagues in a crowded elevator where a patient being transported is treated as invisible, to the discomfort of lying bare backed on a cold radiology table, to a young doctor calling an elderly patient by his or her first name at first meeting, to being cleaned of feces by two individuals discussing their plans for the weekend, to referring to a patient by their pathology ("the gall bladder in 312") rather than their name, the respect with which a patient is treated is often as important as the purely medical treatment they receive. The key, I gradually came to realize, was to understand that my sole reason to be in a hospital was to *care* for patients.

I had spent most months taking call every third night, but in Febru-ary I was assigned to the Neurosurgical Service where I was on duty every other. During that month, I would arrive at the hospital at 5:30 am, then spend the day, the night, and the following day working non-stop, finally getting home at around 8 or 9 pm. Rinse, repeat fifteen times. The nights I took call, I averaged only a few hours' sleep, and on many occasions never went to bed at all. By the end of February, I decided that this kind of life was no life at all, and I began to consider leaving surgery training and switching to Emergency Room Medicine.

By chance, in March I was assigned to the ICU, which was run by the Anesthesia Department. One day the Chairman of Anesthesia, Dr. Buck Wiggers, surprised me by saying, "David, rumor has it you're thinking of leaving surgery and considering Emergency Medicine. You really ought to think about Anesthesia. Come see me in my office."

When we met, I was embarrassed to admit that I knew very little about the practice of anesthesia, despite spending the better part of a year separated from it by only a pinned up sterile drape. Dr. Wiggers described a specialty in which I could put to use many of the components of medicine I had spent so much time learning at LSU—physiology, pharmacology, anatomy, and much more. He said that anesthesiologists were the ICU doctors of the Operating Room. Although some anesthetists described their life as "ninety-nine per cent boredom and one per cent sheer terror," Dr. Wiggers assured me that the specialty was challenging and rewarding, and anything but boring.

One week later, following another discussion and a lot of soul searching, I told Dr. Wiggers I was ready to move to anesthesia. He told me he knew the Chairmen of the best programs in America and that he would call around to see who might have an opening. He listed the locations of each, and I asked about the University of California in San Diego, thinking the weather would be pretty good there. He said it was a top five program and would undoubtedly be filled, but he would call just in case. Later that day, I answered a page to his office. When his secretary answered the phone, she announced cheerfully, "You're going to San Diego." Somehow, they had had a doctor cancel his commitment for the residency just a few days earlier. That sequence of events is typical of how so much in medicine is done, whether it's securing a position in a training program, obtaining a job, or getting plugged in to a professional organization. Someone knows someone, a call is made, and you're in. Ironically, I would be going to one of the best anesthesia programs in the United States, and my sole criteria for choosing it was that on most days the average temperature there was in the 70s.

That night, standing outside the VA Hospital where I was on call, I told Joyce the good news, "We're going to San Diego!" She replied, quickly, "No, you're going to San Diego. I'm not coming with you if we're not married. You should know by now." She then turned abruptly and walked away. She was right. Three months later we were married, and we moved out to California together.

My fascination with the heart never left me, so after my anesthesia residency, I stayed on for an additional year fellowship to specialize in cardiothoracic anesthesia. At the end of August 1980, thirteen days after Joyce delivered our first child, we moved to Nashville, Tennessee to join a private practice group. The hospital I would work at was third busiest in the nation for cardiac surgery, and I wanted to get back to the South, so it seemed like a perfect fit.

In Nashville it seemed there were churches on every corner. It wasn't at all unusual to be in the OR and have a patient request a prayer prior to being put under. The surgeon invariable led the prayer—I wouldn't know where to begin—and I found that patients who faced a dreadful diagnosis or a frightful surgery were somehow comforted by the surgeon's words. Also, Joyce was a committed Christian, and she seemed to be more at peace with the world than I. What do they have that I don't, I wondered?

LIKE ALMOST ALL DOCTORS, I began to really learn only after I left my specialty training. Within a few weeks, and much to my surprise, I encountered patients with problems that I had never confronted. In just about all residencies, you learn how to manage many common conditions, but many more are so infrequent you never come across them. And until you've seen them and dealt with them, you know only *of* them, you don't really know *them*. In addition, there were problems or disorders I didn't even recognize as such, a deficiency alluded to in the often-used medical expression, "You don't know what you don't know." Those were the ones you sometimes learned about the hard way.

The same concepts apply to technical procedures. If you hadn't been taught it during your residency or fellowship, you had to learn it from someone you worked with. There's a phrase almost all medical students and doctors use in a sarcastic way to describe how new skills are acquired: "see one, do one, teach one." It's as if even the most complicated or hazardous procedure is so easy that you not only could perform it having seen it done only once, but you also could be proficient enough after your first experience that you would be ready to impart your newfound skill to someone else. Hardly. It also suggests the importance of having the right expertise around you to facilitate learning the new skill.

There is another expression anesthesiologists often use when they make fun of surgeons who have little experience with an operation but won't admit it. We jokingly use it to describe ourselves, as well. If you've done something a single time, you could tell a patient, "Well, in my experience..." If you've done something twice, you might say, "Well, in case after case, I've found . . . " And after you've done it three times, "Well, in my series of patients . . . " Of course, an ethical doctor would never actually use those expressions with patients, but the fact remains that we never like admitting that we're often on the steep part of the learning curve.

I would never lie to a patient about a lack of experience, but like most doctors, I rarely offered the information spontaneously. It was hard enough to do something I didn't feel totally comfortable with, and even more so if a patient had his or her own reservations. But if pressed for details, brutal honesty was required. If a patient didn't receive that, regardless of specialty, they had the wrong doctor taking care of them.

Early in my practice, with all I still had to learn, I found patients gave me their complete trust almost immediately. Meeting most patients in the holding area or in an outpatient room outside the OR, I usually had no more than ten or fifteen minutes to establish the doctor-patient relationship. In that time period, they were asked to develop confidence that this total stranger would take them closer to death than they would ever come in this life, then bring them safely back.

There were four levels of general anesthesia, which I likened to going on a submarine journey. As you break the surface, Stage 1 takes you from being awake to losing consciousness. Descending, you move through Stage 2, also called the "stage of excitement." At that level, patients could respond to stimuli in exaggerated ways, such as reflexively shutting their vocal cords to prevent breathing. It was the level of anesthesia where you had to bring the submarine lower without provocation. When the sub travels deeper, you arrive at stage 3, the stage of surgical anesthesia at which operations could be performed. You had to be careful not to descend further. At stage 4, the ship would crash on the ocean floor, and death would come quickly. That was the part of giving an anesthetic that frightened me the most. Emergence from anesthesia was merely bringing the ship back to the surface and docking in port.

I sometimes wonder if patients would be so trusting if they knew how much we still don't know about general anesthesia. It's hard to imagine a field of medicine with as large an impact where the basic mechanism of its action is so poorly understood. We know that anesthesia works, but we don't know precisely *how* it works. All we know for certain is that it puts you to sleep in a magical and reversible way. And not only you. Animals, reptiles, fish, and insects are all predictably anesthetized with our agents. The notorious Venus flytrap insect-catching plant is rendered helpless when exposed to our gases. Even plant seed germination ceases under the influence of the vapors patients breathe to render them unconscious. And yet, all improbably recover when our agents are withdrawn.

I don't know how belief in your doctor happens, other than to think that the alternative for a patient—to proceed fearfully with suspicion—is intolerable. Or perhaps it's because we all grow up taught to embrace health professionals as completely honest. Surveys consistently show that doctors are the second most trusted profession in America, bested only by nurses.

After a few years in Nashville, I found myself attracted to working with pain management, but like most anesthesiologists, I had little formal training in it. Fortunately, I had a seasoned older partner, Dr. Bob Martin, who taught me to do most of the procedures I'd never learned as a resident. But not all of them.

One day I was working in the Pain Clinic and saw Mrs. Moscowitz, a patient who suffered from pain radiating into the index and long finger of her right hand. She had been specifically referred to Dr. Martin, but he was on vacation, so that left me to get her ready for his return. Mrs. Moscowitz was a middle-aged woman who required a series of three cervical epidural injections, each spaced apart by a week or two. You likely know how anesthesiologists place epidurals in the lower back of new mothers in labor to assist with their delivery. Labor epidurals are quite safe and easy to do, though if the needle goes in too far it can puncture the membrane that holds in the cerebrospinal fluid (or CSF, the fluid in which the spinal cord floats), which can cause a severe headache. But because the spinal cord ends just above the point where labor epidurals are placed, needles that travel in too deep rarely cause serious nerve injury.

A cervical epidural done for pain is similar, except it's done up in the neck, and a steroid medication is given to reduce inflammation around an irritated nerve root traveling into the arm. As with labor epidurals, a needle inserted too deep will enter the spinal fluid and cause a ferocious headache. But that needle can also pierce the spinal cord, a devastating occurrence that can result in quadriplegia, and in the worst scenario, death. In fact, one of my partners had had a malpractice suit from causing quadriplegia in a man where a needle slipped in too deep, a nightmare for both him and his patient. What's more, even if a practitioner is doing the procedure correctly, the same complication can occur if a patient suddenly flinches and jerks the neck backwards.

The great majority of anesthesiologists never do a cervical epidural in their entire career, primarily because the procedure carries such significant risk. I had not yet done one, though I had seen Dr. Martin place a few. I looked forward to having him with me when I did my first.

Mrs. Moscowitz walked in gingerly, with her right arm hanging down and her left hand grasping her right elbow, as if to keep it from moving too much. She seemed bright and intelligent, with eyes that were focused and attentive. She appeared to be in her late 40s and was well dressed, as if to go out to eat at a fine restaurant. She carried a little more weight than I suspect she wished, but somehow it just seemed to make her look healthy. In addition, she had her bouffant hair teased up high, defying gravity, magically held up in the air like a woven bird's nest. She had a kind of all-American look, sort of like Annette Funicello from those beach movies, only twenty years later. I immediately liked her.

I told Mrs. Moscowitz that Dr. Martin was off that week, but since she had been sent over, I would take her history, examine her, and get her all set up for when he returned. After doing a brief physical exam, I went over the procedure with her, describing how it would be done, what results she might expect, and then the potential complications. In medicine, doctors who do procedures generally disclose the very worst that can occur, even though the risk is remote, just in case. So, I finished my discussion by mentioning the rare occurrence of quadriplegia from a needle going in too far. I don't recall if I included death as an even more remote possibility; the inability to move your arms and legs for the rest of your life was bad enough. Mrs. Moscowitz listened attentively. Then, without hesitation, she asked, "Well, do you want to do it since you're here today?"

I caught my breath and swallowed. I didn't immediately respond. Mrs. Moscowitz must have recognized my hesitation. She added, "How many of these have you done?"

It was a kind of relief she asked me that. I had long contemplated doing my first cervical epidural, and it had long worried me. Maybe if she knew of my inexperience, she would wait for Dr. Martin.

I answered, meekly, "Well, you would be my first." It was half confession and half embarrassed admission. The "see one, do one, teach one" expression was hardly amusing for procedures that carried potentially devastating complications. I wasn't sure I was ready to walk that high tightrope alone, without an experienced teacher like Dr. Martin holding a net underneath. I took a breath and told her how I had seen several placed, that I had done literally hundreds by the lumbar approach, and that I felt reasonably confident that I could do it successfully. But I also reminded her again that potential complications were far more serious when working in the neck. I wished secretly, almost desperately, for her to wait for Dr. Martin's return, but I was too unsettled to admit my preference.

Had I been in her shoes, I might have waited for Dr. Martin. Instead, somehow, inexplicably, she trusted my competence. Without hesitation, she cocked her head and stated, "Well, I'm game if you're up to it." I swallowed hard and summoned one of the nurses for assistance.

Before we even got started, I thought, *man, don't go in too far!* The nurse and I positioned Mrs. Moscowitz sitting on a chair in a treatment room, bent forward, her neck bowed upwards, her head tilted downwards resting on her arms folded on a table in front of her. Standing at her left side, I washed off her skin with an antiseptic and placed a sterile drape. Then I pressed firmly on the bones that ran down her neck along the midline behind her skull, feeling each prominence, or spinous process. I felt for the lower most prominent one, right at the base of her neck, which the anatomy books described as the seventh cervical vertebra. By then, my armpits felt wet. I looked down and saw small rings of perspiration. I paused and tried to slow my breathing. Easy now. In, then out.

I counted up a space and placed a local anesthetic in the skin between the 5th and 6th cervical vertebra—"a little bee sting, here"—and grasped the epidural needle. These needles have a relatively blunt end and a generous diameter. In fact, at what we call 17 gauge, they are far wider than most house framing nails, and at three and a half inches, much longer. They look mean. The blunt tip is designed to allow gradual penetration of the firm membranous layers between the spinal processes—the bones in the neck—and then snap through the innermost layer when the epidural space is entered.

I kept the needle out of her sight. I braced myself and pressed the flat tip through the skin with a kind of "pop." Then I gripped the needle tip firmly where it entered the skin, holding it between my first finger and thumb of my left hand. I advanced the needle inwards, slowly, cautiously, limiting its forward movement to only a fraction of an inch with each push. In my right hand I held a syringe filled with a mixture of air and salt-water solution that I attached to the already inserted needle. As I inched the needle further inwards, a tiny bit followed by a tiny bit, my right thumb gently pushed on the plunger over and over. The plunger descended just a millimeter or two as the air within the syringe was compressed, and then retreated back out each time I relaxed my thumb. The textbooks taught that when you reached the epidural space, the resistance to the thumb would suddenly vanish, and the plunger would easily inject the saline into the space.

I got in around an inch deep—*don't go in too far!*—then stopped. I felt my heart pounding. Surely, I should be there by now, I thought. From Dr. Martin, I knew that in some patients the actual epidural space could be deceptively difficult to identity. Was I already there and didn't know it? If I advanced further, would it be too deep?

Think back, if you're old enough, to your high school biology class. Back in the 1960s and 1970s, students were taught to dissect frogs, and prior to doing so the animals had to be killed. It was considered to be most humane to do so by jamming a needle into the brain at the base of their skull, an action called "pithing." As you did it, the legs and arms of the frog would reflexively jerk outwards in a death spasm, an image that was unforgettable. I couldn't get that picture out of my mind as I pondered what to do.

I can't afford to be wrong, I thought. I pulled the needle out. I said, "I'm going to go in again at a little different angle. Am I hurting you at all?"

"No, I'm fine," Mrs. Moscowitz replied in a muffled voice, her face still buried in her folded arms.

I moved the needle approach slightly and advanced again, just as slowly. I got to that inch depth again. *Don't go in too far!* I breathed in deeply and let it out slowly. I pushed inwards one additional time, to get the needle just a tiny bit deeper. All at once, I felt the plunger of the syringe give way, and I knew I was there. I took a huge breath and exhaled loudly, loud enough that Mrs. Moscowitz must have heard it. She made a little squeaky sound, as if sharing my relief, but said nothing. I took a second syringe and injected the steroid slowly. Then I pulled the needle out as if I were yanking the ripcord of a parachute. I was ecstatic. But I was also relieved that Dr. Martin would do the next two planned blocks.

I applied a band-aide over the needle insertion site and pulled off the sterile drape. Mrs. Moscowitz sat upright, turned, and looked up at me. She was smiling. She chirped, "Well, that went really well. Why don't I come back and have you do the other two?"

As I nodded in ascent, I thought of the expression that "no good deed goes unpunished." I wrote a quick note in the chart and made an appointment for Mrs. Moscowitz to return. "I'll see you at 2 p.m. two weeks from today."

As she walked out of the Clinic, she still held her right arm still. I sat down at a desk and picked up the chart for my next patient. But I could already feel my apprehension about repeating the block. At the same time, I felt wonderful.

I've thought often of how Mrs. Moscowitz trusted me to do a procedure that carried grievous consequences, even though I'd never done it before. Looking back, I wonder if I shouldn't have waited for Dr. Martin to return to guide me through it. Like many of my "firsts" in medicine, I'm just grateful it went well.

Throughout my career, I struggled with judging the moment when I was qualified to do something on my own, whether it was as trivial as sewing up a superficial laceration, or as complex as placing a needle deep inside the body to destroy nerves in a cancer patient suffering pain. When had I seen enough of them to do one with supervision, when was it safe to proceed without a teacher next to me, and when was I qualified to teach others the skill? For many procedures, there were no easy answers. When I was able to, I relied on the mentors who imparted their judgment to me. But just as often, I had to figure it out on my own, as I did with Mrs. Moscowitz.

For my entire career, with all the new things I needed to learn along the way, I never lost my wonder at how quickly patients gave me their trust. There were days when I was so taken by their faith in me that I found myself thinking, I can't believe I get paid to do this job. The faith they showed in me, day after day, year after year, is given to almost all physicians. It is one of the greatest rewards of our profession, and a building block of the doctor-patient relationship. On the doctor's side of the equation, of course, is the understanding of what a privilege it is to treat people who believe in you completely. But this is their *life* they're trusting you with. Can you ever live up to that trust completely?

Chapter 5

GRATITUDE

ONE EVENING EARLY IN my private practice, I answered a STAT call to the Medical ICU. "They need you right away in MS-14 for an intubation." This meant I would need to put a breathing tube into a patient on an urgent basis.

"On my way," I replied.

The emergency requests to place breathing tubes were the ones that made me most fearful. Especially calls like this one, when I was the only anesthesiologist in the hospital. Many times, the summons was made at the last minute, when a patient was just about to give out. That didn't matter much if you were dealing with a small, elderly woman without any teeth, where you could pass the tube seemingly with your eyes closed. On the other end of the spectrum were large male patients, where trying to intubate them could be dangerous even in the best of circumstances.

I ran up two flights of stairs to the ICU and burst through the door. One of the respiratory therapists was stationed outside 14, motioning me in.

The patient looked to be in his late 50s, heavyset, sitting bolt upright in bed. I had learned long ago that position made marginal breathing easier, because patients were better able to expand their lungs without their abdomen pushing up too much. But this man was bluish in color, sweating profusely, greasy hair matted to his scalp, gripping the bedside rails like a drunken sailor trying to keep himself from pitching overboard. His eyes were wide open, and he looked directly ahead, as if staring down his impending demise. His respirations were fast, maybe 45 or 50 times per minute, way over our cut-off rate for needing an ETT and a ventilator. Each breath made a gurgling sound, announcing the in and out of his respirations. Over his nose and mouth, a normally tight-fitting clear plastic facemask sat askew, pulled to one side by the oxygen hose stretched taut to the flow meter on the wall. The mask was meant to deliver 100 percent oxygen, but it had to sit precisely on his face to be effective. His hospital gown had come untied, and it had slid awkwardly down to his elbows, stuck against them with sweat. A pulse oximeter chirped out the oxygen saturation level in his blood. In addition to a visual number readout of 82, there was an audible tone that gave an indication of its level: the higher the pitch, the higher the concentration. His had lowered from its usual soprano in the high 90s to an alto in the 80s. That put his oxygen level right on the edge. I glanced up at the monitor. The heart rate was around 120 with the systolic blood pressure hovering in the low 90s. He was close to giving out.

The patient's nurse was young and looked anxious. As I moved to the head of the bed, she offered a brief report. "This is Mr. Anderson, 58 years old. He has liver cancer with mets to the lungs. He came in this morning short of breath and has been going downhill. We're not sure if this is pneumonia or the cancer. He and the family couldn't decide if they would take the step of intubation or not, but now they've decided to, just in case it is pneumonia and he is able to get over that. He's really slipped over the past fifteen minutes, and that's why I called you STAT. I didn't think you'd get here in time."

The situation was heartbreaking. In all likelihood, it was the cancer that had so overwhelmed Mr. Anderson's lungs that he could no longer breathe adequately on his own. If that were the case, he would die in a week or two with a breathing tube in place, mute, on a ventilator, in the sterile coldness of the ICU. It was a kind of Hail Mary pass to believe that this was pneumonia, but the family was clinging to any hope that his condition might be treated and his life prolonged. I wasn't there to judge the wisdom of keeping him going, though.

Mr. Anderson glanced at me momentarily as I leaned in to the bedside. He looked helpless and smelled like a dirty locker room. "I'm Dr. Alfery," I said. "I'm one of the anesthesiologists. They've called me to pass a breathing tube to help you breathe." I wanted to say more, but I couldn't take the time. He nodded slightly but looked away quickly, as if staring out into space might help him concentrate on getting his breath. I doubted that he understood much of what I said.

My airway examination would be crucial in deciding how to proceed. I announced, "I need to look in your mouth as I get ready to pass my tube. Can you open real wide for me?" As I slipped his oxygen mask off, he opened only partially, then instinctively reached up and jerked the mask back onto has face. I didn't get much of a look, but what I did see was disconcerting. His tongue appeared to fill his mouth entirely, and he had prominent upper front teeth that jutted forward in an overbite. Both those findings predicted difficulty in getting a breathing tube inserted. With just the few seconds the mask was off, the oximeter tone had dropped ominously down to a baritone, and the numerical readout fell into the 70's—dangerously low. He had no reserve at all. I asked him to tilt his head backwards, but he ignored my request. I tried lifting his chin up, but he fought me as he struggled for breath, shaking his head violently. When I looked at his neck, it seemed as if his head was buried on his shoulders, like a Halloween pumpkin sitting on a flour sac. A limited ability to extend the head and a short, thick neck were two additional findings that foretold a very difficult intubation. Perhaps it would be impossible. But without that ETT, he would be dead within minutes.

I didn't dare put him fully to sleep as I would any ordinary patient. The tissues around his airway would likely collapse, and there was no guarantee I could breathe for him adequately with an Ambu bag. And I didn't dare paralyze him to relax his muscles for the intubation—the slightest glitch in the procedure after that would kill him. There were a couple of "rescue" techniques available in that scenario, but I had no time to gather the equipment for them.

Mr. Anderson's breathing seemed to slow, and his saturation hovered in the high 70s, meaning that he was close to the end. I raised the head of the bed to around 45 degrees, removed the headboard at the top end, and crawled up on the frame. I leaned forward with my feet on the horizontal metal bar and my shins pressed against the raised metal mattress frame, trying to pull Mr. Anderson back, saying, "I need you to lie back against the mattress in order to pass the tube. I need you to help me."

He struggled against me, wheezing out, "Can't. Can't."

As I wrestled him backwards, I said, "I understand. But in a minute, I will be breathing for you. I have to do this. Please trust me."

I leaned down, balancing on the bed frame, and I got my mouth close to his ear. "I'm going to place a different facemask on you for a few minutes, and then I'm going to ask you to open your mouth as wide as you can so I can pass the breathing tube. I will make you sleepy for this, but it's going to be uncomfortable. There will be a machine to help you breathe when I get done." I pulled him back; he resisted less.

If I could hold the Ambu mask tight against Mr. Anderson's face, it would allow me to get pure oxygen into his lungs, which should get his oxygen concentration up to a safer level. It would also allow me to try, at least, to take over his breathing if he gave out entirely. I clamped the mask tight over his nose and mouth with my left hand, but his sweat prevented a good seal. Still, I tried to assist his breathing by squeezing the Ambu bag with my right hand. I waited for the tone of the oximeter to change. It rose only slightly. The pitch sang out 83. Not good.

I balanced precariously on the bed frame. If I leaned too far forward, I would pitch over onto the patient. If I leaned back, I would fall off. My shins were beginning to burn from the pressure of being jammed against the edge of the frame.

I turned to the nurse, and said, "Let's give him 2 milligrams of Versed." This sedative had a well-known side effect of causing a brief period of amnesia. Two milligrams was a tiny dose for what I was going to do, a brutal intubation with a patient all but awake, but I hoped it would be enough to at least erase the memory.

The nurse drew up an ampule of the drug and twisted the syringe into an injection port of the IV tubing. "Ready," she asked?

Just then, I noticed that Mr. Anderson was moving his mouth, as if chewing on something. He was trying to speak. I leaned over him and briefly released the facemask. He looked up at me with his eyelids fluttering like butterfly wings. He mumbled something indistinct.

I asked, "What are you trying to say?"

He was gasping for air and tried again. I still couldn't understand. The oximeter tone dropped precariously. I reapplied the mask for a few breaths and then removed it again. "Say again?"

He rasped out, "Thank you," mouthing the words as much as voicing them. Then he closed his eyes and his breathing almost stopped.

He was done struggling.

And we were out of time.

I reapplied the mask as I turned to the nurse. "Give it, please." The nurse injected the Versed and opened the IV to get it in quickly. Within seconds, Mr. Anderson ceased breathing entirely. I tried to take over with the Ambu bag and mask but once more couldn't get it to seal because of all the sweat. And as I feared, the tissues in his airway had collapsed, making oxygen delivery to his lungs impossible. I pried open his mouth and placed a curved plastic oral airway inside to bring the tongue off his soft palate and up from the back of his throat. I tried the Ambu bag and mask again. Nothing. The oximeter pitch sank with each heartbeat, now down to the 70s.

My heart raced.

I took my right hand and tried to pry his jaws apart. They were tight, with his teeth clenched, perhaps as a reflex to how low his oxygen level had fallen. I pried harder, grunting with the effort. His jaws wouldn't open much, but just enough to remove the plastic airway and get a laryngoscope blade in (so named because one can see at its tip the larynx, or entry to the trachea). I leaned my head in, my eyes right next to his nose, then slipped the laryngoscope blade along the side of his tongue. The stimulation was enough to get him partly responsive, and he thrashed his head side to side like a fish trying to spit out a hook. His teeth clenched down against the blade, and I pulled it out quickly, before his front incisors would crack against it. An alarm sounded. I looked up at the monitor and the blood pressure hovered just above 80, dropping due to the sedation. The tone of the oximeter dropped further still.

I could give a paralytic agent to relax his muscles and perhaps allow easier insertion of the laryngoscope, but that could kill him, as it would totally eliminate his ability to breathe. Instead, I requested, "Two more milligrams of Versed, please," hoping the sedation would relax the patient enough to allow me to somehow muscle the tube in. The oximeter tones fell into a deep bass. The alarm continued to blare out in time with the heartbeat, warning of a dangerously low oxygen saturation or blood pressure. It didn't matter which it was. My options had narrowed, and for better or worse, my course was set. I tried again to ventilate by mask, again without success.

Once the Versed was in, I re-inserted the laryngoscope blade, and this time it seemed to go in without a struggle. Maybe it was because he was more sedated, or perhaps he was so oxygen deprived he could no longer fight. Or maybe I was so overcome with fear that I had some kind of unusual strength, like those guys you hear about who could suddenly lift a car right off an accident victim. Whatever it was, when I got the blade all the way in, I couldn't see anything but blood and saliva.

I pulled it out and barked, "Suction!" The nurse slapped a stiff plastic catheter into my outstretched right hand. I rammed it into his mouth and pushed it against the back of his throat. A mixture of blood and saliva slurped up. I pulled the catheter out and tossed it to the side.

I stuck the laryngoscope blade back in and slid it down towards his larynx. The patient was not fighting at all. He had the kind of slackness that the newly dead have. At the tip I saw tissue, lots of pink tissue, but nothing I could recognize. Then suddenly, there was the epiglottis, the cartilaginous flap that covers the entrance to the trachea like a garage door. I lifted it up, using all my strength, and I saw just the bottom of the vocal cords. A marginal view, but it might be enough.

The respiratory therapist placed the ETT into my outstretched hand while I kept my eyes fixed on the cords. I slid it past the blade and tried to push it in. It pressed against the vocal cords, but it would not go through. They were reflexively shut due to the stimulation of the laryngoscope blade deep in his throat. I thought again about giving a paralytic agent, this time to open the cords. I could assume that paralysis would now be reasonably safe since I was able to visualize the entrance to the trachea. But what if I somehow lost that visualization and never got it back?

I waited.

I knew that sooner or later the vocal cords would open, but by that time he would be frightfully close to death. My shins were burning, screaming out to back away from the bed frame, but I was locked in position. The room was silent except for the alarm and the oximeter, its pitch rumbling lower still, and sounding more like a groan than a tone. I knew it had to be in the 50s, maybe even lower. You couldn't live more than a couple of minutes at that level. I felt my left arm shaking from muscle fatigue. I was not aware of anything else in the room, my focus tunneled down to just the corridor from my eyes to the closed vocal cords that stood between the patient's life and his death. I tried to calculate how much time I might have before irreversible brain damage occurred. Ninety seconds? Sixty?

And then, just for a second, the cords relaxed and opened a tiny bit. I saw a glimmer of black trachea between them. I shoved the ETT tip up against the slit, hard, but enough to get it started. The bevel at the end of the tube did the rest, prying open the cords so the tube could slide in.

Got you, you bastard!

I quickly removed the laryngoscope blade. I switched from my right hand to my left, holding the ETT in place with a death grip. The respiratory therapist placed the Ambu bag in my right hand and I attached it to the ETT. I squeezed the bag hard, and the chest rose. Within around 20 seconds, the normal lag time for the oximeter to record changes, I heard the tone slightly ascend! And then come up further, faster. I looked at the monitor and saw the reading advance from the 40s, quickly moving up through the 50s, the 60s, the 70s, then into the 80s. I felt a rush of relief, of joy. Thank God! I was happy for the patient, but if I'm completely honest, I was just as happy for myself.

The alarm fell silent.

The rest went quickly.

As the reparatory therapist took over holding the ETT and prepared to tape it into place, I said something like, "I'm going to kill you if you let this tube come out." We both let out a nervous little laugh. I climbed down from the bed frame. The blood pressure had come back up to around 100, likely due to the stimulation of the ETT. Even the oximeter was now in the 90s with our ability to fully expand the patient's lungs. I bent over and rubbed the indented skin at the tops of my shins, trying to massage the pain away.

But my job was done.

I wrote a quick note in the chart. Nothing could describe just how closely Mr. Anderson had come to losing his life. And no words could express my gratitude that the ETT had gone in at the end. I scribbled something like, "#8.0 ETT passed with Versed 4 mg. sedation. Breath sounds bilateral. Saturation 94%. Chest x-ray pending." So much unsaid. I grabbed a face sheet for billing purposes and headed back downstairs.

As I waited for the elevator, I thought for a moment. Unless you lived it, no one would ever understand how terrifying my job could be. Nor could you ever know all I was privileged to experience. Mr. Anderson was dying, whether from his cancer, his pneumonia, or God forbid, my inability to pass the ETT. And chances were, he would never live to have his breathing tube removed. I doubt he fully comprehended what I was doing for him, just that I was an unknown doctor there to try and help. Even during his desperate struggle to hang on, with his last breath, he had the grace to express his gratitude to me. They were likely the last words he ever spoke.

Of course, most of the calls to pass a breathing tube in an ICU patient were for those in whom recovery was expected. But still, I encountered many patients similar to Mr. Anderson during my career, though none in whom I had such terrifying difficulty in passing the ETT. What they had in common was a terminal disease process from which few were likely to recover. The breathing tube and ventilator would buy them a little more time, maybe a few days, maybe a few weeks, but the end was pretty much predetermined. The tube would never be removed, they would never leave their ICU bed, and they would succumb to their illness. Either the family or the patient—or in some cases, their doctor—had thought that some heroic measures might save them, but that would be the exception. For those who were elderly, I could generally do my work without much emotion clouding over me. But for those who were young, say a mother with Stage 4 breast cancer and children still in the house, the poignancy could be overwhelming.

When intubating desperately ill patients who seemed unlikely to survive their hospitalization, I did my best not to be judgmental, and I tried not to put myself in their place. I had seen over and over how many people had difficulty accepting death as it approached. Maybe that was a natural consequence of all the advances in medicine. Maybe it came from seeing stories of amazing recoveries on TV. Maybe it was a result of someone talking to someone who had heard from someone else that recovery was possible in a particular situation. I saw repeatedly that for many—doctors as well as patients—there was some kind of unspoken expectation that we would try to extend life beyond what Nature had in mind.

And who knows what the patient or their family had been told? Were they given false hope? Did they fully comprehend what dying in the cold sterility of an ICU might be like? Did they know what it was like to see a loved one never get that breathing tube taken out, to never get off the ventilator until they passed? Were heroic measures, to continue the fight for life, simply easier—for the patient, for the family, for the doctor treating them—than facing the bitter reality that the end had come? I vowed that if I were ever in a situation of needing intubation when my prognosis was dismal, I would decline the intervention and elect comfort treatment instead. I know that many of my colleagues would do the same. Studies have shown that doctors actually consume fewer medical resources at the end of life than lay people. Still, you never know what decision you'll make until you're there.

The other thing these desperate patients had in common was the kinds of things they said just before the tube was placed. Like Mr. Anderson, I heard, "Thank you" from many. They expressed what I consider to be a key to happiness in life: they voiced gratitude for what they had—a doctor who cared and was there to help them—rather than bitterness over what they did not.

It's an open question if anyone really benefits when we prolong life with little hope of recovery. Maybe we would better spend our energy accepting the end and simply showing love to those about to die, as well as to those with whom we hope to be living for years to come.

Chapter 6

SUFFERING

MOST PEOPLE HAVE HEARD of the Hippocratic Oath. It has been taken by physicians upon entering medicine since the time of the Greeks, and I took it when I graduated from LSU Medical School in 1976. Less known is the Oath of Maimonides, sometimes used as a substitute for the Hippocratic. In fact, it focuses far more on what it means to be a doctor. Dating back to 1793, it reads, in part, "May the love for my art actuate me at all times . . . May I never see in the patient anything but a fellow creature in pain."

Even if they don't work in a formal pain clinic, doctors trained in anesthesia are usually turned to when other physicians have difficulty managing a patient's physical suffering. In my experience, the greatest difficulty most often occurs in cancer patients near the end. Some of these patients receive enormous doses of narcotics, but they have become so tolerant to the medications they obtain little relief.

Our Anesthesia Department received a consult early one afternoon to evaluate and treat a patient on one of the medical wards. Given the location, I figured it was someone with a malignancy. I was free, so I went up to see him, and before heading to the room, I paged through his chart. Mr. Diamond had metastatic colon cancer, with extensive spread to his liver, lungs, pelvis, and spine. He had been admitted two days earlier for control of his pain. Since admission, his oncologist had ordered an infusion of increasing doses of a narcotic called Dilaudid, but it had had little effect. By the time we were called, he was receiving 20 mg./hour, and he was still in agony. I thought, man, that's a big dose. We usually only needed 2—4 mg. every three or four hours after major abdominal surgery. Could we help?

Mr. Diamond's chart was pretty skimpy. He hadn't been in the hospital long, and other than the fact he was rapidly dying, he only had one problem. The history stated that he had stopped eating almost a week prior to admission. He would take a few spoonfuls of liquid, but a day before he came in, he had stopped that. On the day of admission, he was barely able to respond to his family, and then within a few hours that slipped away. All he would do, or could do, it seemed, was lie in pain and moan. He had no fever, but his blood pressure had been gradually slipping lower. He was expected to die in the hospital within a day, two at the most. When I closed the chart, I noted a big red "DO NOT RESUSCITATE" sticker stuck at a 45-degree angle across the front, meaning that he would receive no special life support such as an ETT and ventilator or CPR when death was imminent. I was thankful the decision to make Mr. Diamond a "no code" had been made; it would certainly make my job more straightforward.

I placed the chart in the rack and walked to the very end of the ward. The nurses usually put the most difficult patients all the way down the hallway to better shield others from cries of distress that might come from their rooms.

The door was closed, so I knocked lightly and pushed it slowly inwards. Even before it opened, I heard the patient panting and moaning with each breath, each one coming quickly, maybe thirty times per minute. That alone told me his that Dilaudid was ineffective, as any narcotic should depress and slow breathing down. His moan with each breath was brief, wavering, dropping just a little in tone each time he exhaled. It also came with a gurgling sound, as if the air were bubbling up, sputtering up through liquid. All doctors and nurses know that sound. It's called a "death rattle," the breathing noise patients make when they're nearing the end.

Mr. Diamond was lying on his side, facing away from me, slightly curled with his legs bent up. The room was silent and dimly lit, the shades fully closed, as a single light above the bed washed against the wall towards the ceiling.

I announced myself to those present, a wife, two sons, and a daughter-in-law. "Hello. I'm Dr. Alfery. I'm from the Anesthesia Department. Dr. Cook has asked us to come see Mr. Diamond and try to help relieve his pain."

An IV pole stood at the bedside, with two bags hanging from the top. I figured one would be the Dilaudid and the other a carrier fluid. Each fed into an infusion pump, with a single line traveling to Mr. Diamond's arm. A urinary catheter drainage tube emerged from under his blanket and led to a collection bag that was hooked to the bedframe. It was empty. Urination often stopped as death approached. A TV in the far upper corner was on, but the sound was turned off. The wife, who had been lying on a big chair that flattened backwards and whose lower end extended outwards in a futile attempt to make a bed—the hospital's equivalent to a Barcalounger—groaned as she got up slowly. She looked worn out and shell-shocked, as she mumbled that Mr. Diamond was her husband. I extended my hand and felt her limp hand in mine. I gave a gentle squeeze and felt nothing in return.

Three other small chairs had been brought into the room, arranged around the bed as if it was a campfire. A variety of fast-food containers lined the counter under the window, some crumpled. At the end of the counter were a discarded newspaper and some rumpled clothes. In the corner under the TV lay more discarded clothing. The room smelled old and decaying. Mr. Diamond's rhythmic moaning, like a death knell metronome, dominated everything.

None of younger three appeared to have slept much in the past 24 hours, and if they had, it had likely been in fits, slumped in a chair or stretched out on the floor. They wore blue jeans and shirts; mom wore a wrinkled dress. The guys had not shaved in at least a day. They looked to be from the country, outside of Nashville, where people didn't worry too much about the way they dressed. Rural Tennessee folk were generally hard working, but they had far less disposable income than residents of the city, with its music, tourism, and other industries. These country folk were generally tough and independent. From the sound of Mr. Diamond, all the toughness and independence he might have had throughout his life had gone out.

The taller of the two sons stood over me by half a foot. Though physically imposing, he looked fragile. He gripped his hands together, squeezing them, then relaxing, then squeezing again. He cleared his throat and spoke for the group. "We're mighty glad to see you, doctor. My dad is suffering so. We have to do something, anything. We can't have him like this. He just can't bear this." As he spoke, I noticed tears in his eyes.

I shook my head to the side and let out a deep breath. "I'm so sorry for all of you," I said. "And especially for your father. We're going to do our best to get him some relief."

As we discussed Mr. Diamond's rapid descent, the most important thing I learned was that all the family had been able to say their good-byes to Mr. Diamond before he had been admitted. Now, they just wished for his suffering to end.

I moved around the end of the bed to face the patient and said to the son, "I need to do a brief examination."

I looked down at Mr. Diamond. Someone had combed his hair neatly to the side, but he had the appearance common to those approaching death: gaunt, unshaven, face ashen grey, eyes closed, mouth open, drool sliding from its corner. The medical slang for the appearance of an unresponsive patient with the mouth open and the tongue hanging to the side was the "Q-sign." It was a callous description meant to shield those who spoke it from the awful reality of the situation.

I bent over and placed my hand on Mr. Diamond's shoulder. Then I squeezed it firmly and gently shook him, saying, "Mr. Diamond? Mr. Diamond? Can you hear me, Mr. Diamond?"

There was nothing but the moaning.

I reached down and took his right hand in mine. I tried again. "Mr. Diamond, can you squeeze my right hand?" I squeezed mine against his. "Squeeze your hand, Mr. Diamond."

Again, nothing but the moaning.

Finally, I forcefully pinched the skin above his collarbone, a maneuver that is exquisitely painful and would bring any patient out of a deep sleep.

Nothing but the moaning.

The son said, bleakly, "He's been pretty much like this since we got here."

The moaning continued.

I stood up and looked at the family. They looked back with apprehension, even desperation. As was often the case with the loved ones of terminal patients, they needed relief from their suffering more than the patient did.

Rarely were we called to see patients like Mr. Diamond. Either they were in better shape or they'd died by the time anyone thought to consult the Anesthesia Service. I pondered for a moment how to proceed. Desperate times call for desperate measures.

Looking between the taller son and the wife, I said, "I know you're aware that Mr. Diamond is not going to suddenly somehow get better, that he will likely pass within a day, maybe two at the most. I think you can be comforted in that, despite his moans, he likely has no conscious realization of his pain. By that, I mean that if he suddenly awakened and you asked if he had been in pain, he would tell you, no. Still, I think we can make absolutely sure of that."

I paused for a moment for the family to absorb what I was saying. Then I continued. "To accomplish that, we need to start an infusion of a drug called propofol. This is a medicine that can put you lightly to sleep in lower doses and can put you under general anesthesia with higher doses. I think with all the Dilaudid Mr. Diamond is receiving, it won't take much to reduce his moaning, but whatever the dose he needs, we can give it."

I paused again, then added, "At that point, there will be no chance of his responding to any of you in any way. He will be even more deeply asleep than he is right now. You do have to know, though, that every drug he receives, just like his Dilaudid, depresses his breathing and interferes with his ability to do the most basic things we take for granted. Things like coughing when we need to. So even his pain medicine is likely moving him along to passing a little faster than he would otherwise go. Our propofol will add to that."

The discourse I gave them was an attempt to explain the relationship between pain and consciousness, between being in misery and knowing you are in misery. Everyone feels pain, and the greater the pain, as well as the more awake a person is, the greater the suffering. But if you depress consciousness to the point where a patient is not aware of anything around them, where they can no longer respond to the voice of a loved one because they are too asleep to hear it, their body still responds to the pain. It does so by writhing back and forth or by moaning. Those are elemental reactions that a patient is unaware of, just as one is unaware of turning over in bed when asleep or what goes on under anesthesia. The moaning and writhing are nevertheless agonizing for a family to witness. That was where Mr. Diamond was—unaware and unconscious of his suffering—but with his family fully experiencing it.

"Do you understand what I've said and what I am suggesting we do?" I asked.

The taller son exhaled deeply, and his shoulders slumped. His face relaxed slightly. It seemed whatever burden he had been carrying had been at least partly lifted from his shoulders. He spoke again for the family, almost pleading, "Doctor, we want you to do everything possible to make sure he's not in pain."

I took his hand and shook it. "I will. Again, I'm so sorry y'all are going through this. It's going to take a little time to get this going, maybe an hour or more, but we'll go as fast as we can."

As I left the room, the family was looking back and forth at each other, maybe still trying to fully comprehend what I'd told them. Most families in situations such as theirs understood only the most basic parts of an explanation.

I went to the nurse's station and ordered that a propofol infusion be set up, then told his floor nurse I would be back to help get it going.

An hour later I returned, just as the infusion was being hung on the IV pole. I drew some propofol from its glass container into a syringe. Whatever dose I gave, it would be a balancing act. Any more than I needed to quiet him would likely kill him. I injected 10 mg, a very small amount, then waited. Within a couple of minutes Mr. Diamond's moaning had softened. I injected another 10 mg, and his moaning stopped entirely, abruptly. His breathing slowed way down and almost ceased. Had I given too much? I silently wished I'd given only 5 mg. But the total amount he'd received would barely register with a patient who was wide-awake.

Thankfully, Mr. Diamond's breathing steadied and picked back up. It was mildly slower than when I had met him, but there was no moaning, only the sound of the gurgling of air moving in and out. I breathed a sigh of relief. I calculated the infusion rate that I thought was appropriate and asked the nurse to start it. "I'll be back a couple of times before I go home tonight," I told her, "and you know you just need to call the 850 beeper to get the anesthesiologist on call. But our objective here, the dose we are aiming for, is the dose that just stops his moaning." She nodded her assent. There was no specific science that told me the endpoint of treatment should be cessation of moaning, and you wouldn't find advice on treating patients in as desperate shape as Mr. Diamond in any textbooks. Administering propofol to that level just seemed a reasonable stopping point, and it was a clinical state that a floor nurse could easily understand.

I turned to the family. Each member wore an expression of enormous relief. Their suffering was ending. The son pumped my hand and thanked me. I told him I'd be back to check on his father, but we could all be certain that he was totally out of pain.

I came back twice before leaving for the night. Each time, the wife was sitting on her makeshift bed, holding Mr. Diamond's hand. She looked brighter, stronger, like she had somehow rallied. The others were talking quietly, seeming content and accepting. Mr. Diamond's breathing had slowed further, but the moaning had not returned. I left a note in our anesthesia office that I would see our pain patients in the morning, rather than be assigned general post-op visits, in order to look in on Mr. Diamond.

The next day I arrived at the hospital a little early, thinking I might need some extra time in Mr. Diamond's room. I went up to his floor and walked to the end of the hall. The door was open, and the room was empty. The bed was made up, and all the trash had been discarded.

I went back to the nurse's station and found his night nurse, getting ready to go home. She knew why I was there.

"Dr. Alfery, what you guys did was amazing. Mr. Diamond was suffering so, and that propofol made him so peaceful. And the family could finally rest and let the burden of his pain go. I think the propofol helped them as much as it did Mr. Diamond. He passed right around 2 am with his wife and the older son there. They seemed to be relieved when he passed, more than anything else. When they left at around 2:30, the son told me, "You'll never know what you did for my dad. We are so grateful.""

I got a lump in my throat as she spoke. What I did was nothing extraordinary, really. The family was in agony, even if Mr. Diamond only looked that way. It was most humane to treat everyone in the room, and I had the skills to do it. Any of my partners could have done the same.

I thanked the nurse and hurried off to see our other pain patients.

How we deal with pain and suffering at the end of life is challenging. There's usually a balancing act between relieving a patient's suffering while still trying to allow them enough consciousness—to be awake enough—to interact with their family in a meaningful way. Often, as with Mr. Diamond, it is impossible to accomplish both. For almost everyone, the relief of pain trumps everything else. How far you go to accomplish that, though, is where controversy lies.

The professional ethics I worked under required me to act with beneficence, to do what was best for the patient. For Mr. Diamond, that meant treating his pain. But one could argue that he most likely wasn't truly experiencing the pain he appeared to be in. The second medical principle I was supposed to follow was called non-maleficence, that it was more important to not harm a patient than to do them good. Unfortunately, the propofol would depress his respirations and worsen his condition. When two basic ethics were in conflict with each other, I was taught that you should follow the one you felt was more important. I opted for administering propofol.

I'm not certain the ethics fell to giving it, but it felt like the right thing to do. What I did was in no way an attempt to hasten Mr. Diamond's death, though it probably did so. Euthanasia, while legal in some European countries, went against everything I believed a doctor should do. I simply saw him as a fellow creature in pain and treated him as best I could.

Of equal importance, as I made my decision, I saw a family in pain. It was wives, and sons, and daughters-in-law like Mr. Diamond's that taught me the importance of recognizing the distress in those around the patients I cared for. When I met with a patient, I looked for anguish in the family members that were present, as well, and as much as I could, I tried to alleviate their anxiety and address their needs as much as those of the patient. The endpoint of Mr. Diamond's treatment was the alleviation of his family's suffering, and that coincided with Mr. Diamond entering a sleep deep enough to stop his moaning.

Being mindful of a family's needs is far more difficult in today's practice of medicine. Everyone—doctors, nurses, aides, technicians—is being asked to do more in less time. Some busy physicians might not discuss a patient's care with the family for several days if those loved ones are not right in the room when the doctor makes rounds. It's not intentional, but simply a byproduct of the time pressure put on all health care workers. I don't know how that is best addressed, other than to ask your doctor that he or she slow down enough to include everyone in the care plan. Doctors all want to do that, but sometimes they need to be gently reminded. When physicians receive that request, almost all will be grateful to be pulled back to that basic tenant of medical care, the one that Maimonides had challenged us with years ago.

Chapter 7

*F*AITH

DURING MY FIRST YEARS of practice, each Sunday Joyce would take our young daughters to church with her while I played racquetball with a friend. I sometimes wondered how she felt being the only adult Christian in our household. Now I realize she was just living as if she were the first Christian in the home. Over time, I sensed a kind of emptiness within me, even though I had all the material things I wanted. Also, I recognized more and more that in my life, both in and outside of medicine, I had only the illusion of control. No matter how hard I tried, no matter how much I thought I did things right, factors beyond me dictated much of what occurred. I started reading books about Christianity and talking about faith with physician friends for whom religion was a central part of their lives. I went to see the pastor of Joyce's church, and over several years we met repeatedly in his office.

Even with financial security, doctors are not immune to the kind of mid-life restlessness I was experiencing. Some respond to those feelings by buying an expensive car, others take exotic vacations, while still others get a girlfriend on the side. I got baptized.

Following my conversion, prayer became a central part of my spiritual life. Each day, I would drive into the physician's parking lot around 6:15 am and turn off the engine. I would close my eyes and fold my hands, then pray for my family, for individuals that I knew were in need, and for other things in my life. But I always ended up with a prayer for the patients I would care for that day, that they would have a smooth and successful anesthetic and surgery.

I was never the kind of physician to push prayer on my patients. But when the circumstances seemed appropriate for sharing my faith, I didn't hesitate. Typically, this would be when I found a pastor accompanying a patient for my pre-operative interview or when a patient said something like, "My whole church has been praying for me." In those times, I always said the same thing: "I've already prayed for you today." I told them of my morning routine, though I didn't know exactly who my patients would be until I walked into the OR and learned my assignment for the day. The patients invariably responded with remarks like, "Well, the Lord knew exactly whom you were praying for," or, simply, "Thank you." My words in those situations seemed to be hugely comforting for patients of faith.

One day in one of the cardiovascular holding rooms I met Mr. Phillips, along with his wife and pastor. He was a 50-year-old patient scheduled for a routine heart revascularization. He was lying on his stretcher with the sheet pulled up to mid-chest level and the head of the bed tilted up around thirty-five degrees. He looked to be no more than forty, totally fit and athletic, seemingly more suited to having surgery for a sports injury than for coronary blockages. He was buoyant and optimistic, friendly and outgoing, with a quick smile. He was easy to interact with, and I immediately connected with him.

Mr. Phillips, like everyone I took care of, was pre-op'd with the same routine used by just about all doctors, regardless of specialty, when they encounter a new patient. In successive steps we take a history, do a physical examination, check laboratory or other available studies, and then make a plan. For Mr. Phillips, the history entailed learning the particulars that had caused him to need his operation, as well as any other medical history that might be pertinent, such as heavy cigarette smoking in the past or any major illnesses that might affect his care. Mr. Phillips had been remarkably free of disease until his heart got into trouble. Also with the history, I asked about any medications he took or any allergies to drugs. Mr. Phillips replied that he took no medications and had never reacted adversely to a drug.

Following the history, I did a focused physical examination. Most physicians do a physical examination tailored to their specialty. I paid particular attention to his airway—the condition of his teeth, how well he could open his mouth, the size of his tongue, how well he could tilt his head back, and so forth—to assure myself I would not have any difficulty with his breathing (for example, in placing the breathing tube). Mr. Phillips' airway was normal. For patients who were going to have a spinal or epidural anesthetic, a look at the lower back was warranted. Finally, I listened to (or auscultated, the medical term for listening, done with a stethoscope) his lungs and heart. For young healthy patients, and even for Mr. Phillips, that part of the examination was more a formality than a necessity. For older patients, listening to lung sounds would alert me to the presence of wheezing or could point to a problem with the heart. The heart was auscultated primarily to listen for a "murmur," the sound turbulent blood makes going through a valve or narrowed opening. Some murmurs are "innocent," or normal. Other pathologic murmurs reflect disease—such as a sticky cardiac valve. Regardless of a patient's age, I always placed my left hand on the patient's shoulder (when doctors touch a patient in this way, it is referred to as "laying on of hands") when I listened to the heart and lungs, believing that tactile gesture somehow strengthened the bond between the patient and me. I did that with Mr. Phillips, and as expected, heard nothing abnormal when I listened to his chest.

I moved on to the third part of my pre-op, checking any laboratory or radiologic imaging studies that had been done. For a cardiac case, I wanted to know what the heart catheterization showed, how well the muscle was pumping, and if there were any cardiac valve abnormalities present. Fortunately, Mr. Phillips' only problem was the arterial blockages that his surgeon was going to address.

My final step was to come up with an anesthetic plan, describe it to Mr. Phillips, and then obtain an "informed consent." In theory, I was supposed to discuss the anesthetic options with a patient, the advantages and disadvantages of each, as well as any potential risks or complications with each. I usually abbreviated the options discussion and simply gave my recommendation of which technique I favored. Legally, the complications that were to be covered were what any "prudent" person would want to know. Frankly, there was no way of knowing what that might be for any given patient. Many anesthesiologists felt that the complications to be mentioned were those that were most common (such as nausea), those that were uncommon but troublesome (such as a broken tooth), or those that were the most serious, even if they were rare (stroke, death, etc.). Since all our patients signed an anesthetic consent form that listed almost twenty complications, my usual informed consent went something like this: "I think we should do a general anesthetic for this operation. One minute you will be vaguely aware of what is going on, and then the next thing you'll remember will be some time after surgery is finished. There are lots of potential complications with anesthesia, and they were listed on the consent form you signed. If you read it carefully, it looks like we're going to try to kill you. We're not going to do that. In fact, general anesthesia has never been safer. I expect you to do great. Do you have any questions?" I gave Mr. Phillips something pretty close to that routine presentation.

I went through this standard regimen with Mr. Phillips in less than fifteen minutes, along with giving him some of the details of the monitoring lines I would place and how he would wake up in the ICU very gradually, unable to speak, with a machine helping him breathe. As usual, I did the pre-op as quickly as I could, knowing I had other duties awaiting me, but not so fast that he would feel short changed. I finished by telling Mr. Phillips that he was very low risk and stated again that I expected him to do well.

He replied, "Well, my whole church is praying for me, so I believe I will do well."

I responded quickly, as if it were prerecorded. "Well, I've already prayed for you today." Then I briefly described to him my morning routine.

Mr. Phillips looked up. His eyes were glistening. He said, "Thank you. Thank you, so much." His wife, standing by the bedside and holding his hand, murmured her thanks, as well.

The anesthetic was straightforward, done as I had in cardiac cases several thousand times before. On the surface, giving a general anesthetic is easy. Just give more to get the patient more fully asleep. Turn it off at the end, and the patient eventually awakens. Knowledge of the all the variables at play is the science part. There is also the part we call the "art," deciding *how* to combine our various drugs to make the witches brew that will render a patient properly anesthetized. That's where things get complicated and where individual practitioners differ.

Start with the myriad drug options available to us. Then think about how the drugs interact with each other and how doses are so dependent on the age and condition of the patient. Throw in the illnesses a patient might bring with them to surgery. Take into account the fact that they haven't eaten in hours, and don't forget to factor in any blood loss or evaporative fluid loss from, say, an open belly during surgery. Make sure the urine output is adequate and regulate that body temperature. Anticipate the amount of pain after surgery and get the right dose of analgesic on board. All that, and we haven't even gotten to the complexity that surgery itself adds. For those who put people to sleep for operations, there are as many drug combinations and doses available as there are ways to make gumbo in Louisiana—plenty. The science is knowing the facts, the art is the doing. Doing it is harder than it looks.

After we got Mr. Phillips to sleep, I slid an echocardiogram probe into his esophagus, and the image projected on the monitor screen showed his heart beating without any abnormality whatsoever. Very vigorous, the entire muscle moving as expected, only it needed a little more blood going to it when it would be working hard. Our routine cardiac operation would provide that.

The surgeon, Dr. Sandy Pickins, sewed the distal ends of the vein grafts onto the heart vessels with the heart motionless, arrested by a cold preservative solution. When he removed the cross clamp from the aorta and restored blood flow to the heart, I expected it to resume beating within a few minutes. Instead, it lay in the chest, flaccid, unmoving. It looked limp and pale, seemingly lifeless. The appearance was similar to a wet football that had been deflated. I knew from experience that failure to resume beating on its own was an ominous sign, an indication that the cardiac muscle had not been supplied enough oxygen and energy during the time the bypass grafts were being placed. Dr. Pickins and I looked at each other. He furrowed his brow. We each knew what the other was thinking.

Dr. Pickins silently attached pacemaker wires to the surface of the heart and passed the ends over the ether screen to me. I plugged them into a pacemaker box and turned it on, delivering a small current to the upper and lower chambers of the heart. That started the heart contracting, but only weakly. The lower muscular chambers, the ventricles, barely moved. I fiddled with the pacemaker settings to make sure the impulse from the upper chamber was passing to the lower, the way it should be. No dice. That was another worrisome sign.

"He's blocked," I reported. "We're going to have to A-V pace him."

Dr. Pickins shook his head back and forth. He looked down and made a low guttural sound, a kind of half grunt and half clearing his throat. Neither of us was happy.

He silently leaned over the chest cavity and spent the next twenty minutes sewing the proximal ends of the grafts to the aorta, establishing blood flow through them. We waited for the added blood flow to help the heart recover. Even after another twenty minutes, the ventricles were barely moving as they attempted to squeeze.

"I don't get it," Dr. Pickins wondered aloud. "We got a great arrest right away, and there was no activity during the grafting. Maybe some blockages prevented the 'plegia from getting all the way in? I wonder if I should have done retrograde?" he added. Retrograde cardioplegia was an alternative way to get the high potassium arresting fluid into the cardiac muscle, to push it in backwards from the venous side and avoid the extensive obstructions in his native cardiac vessels. Sandy and I were both wishing he had done so.

The mood in the room shifted from casual to somber. I briefly thought about my prayer discussion several hours earlier, but I moved on to focus on the problem at hand.

As a routine case, the patient should have been able to separate from bypass without the assistance of any medications. There was no way that was going to happen with Mr. Phillips.

"Well, I'm going to give him some extra juice," I said reassuringly, though I didn't feel that way myself.

Without discussion, my cardiac Certified Registered Nurse Anesthetist (CRNA), Lela Hanson, increased the rate of epinephrine we were giving, while I opened an ampule of a drug called milrinone. Both those agents would help the heart contract more vigorously. I injected the milrinone in over five minutes and then added two additional infusions, one to further improve the muscle squeezing, and the other to help adjust the resistance against which it beat. It looked like all of those would be needed if we were to have Mr. Phillips get off the heart bypass machine.

After another ten-minute period of drug infusion, Dr. Pickins told the perfusionist to allow the heart to receive some blood back into it, so we could assess how well it beat while filled as opposed to being empty. It looked dreadful. I looked over to Dr. Pickins. He looked dreadful, too. There is a lonely place surgeons occupy when they have operated on patients in relatively good health and their procedure has made them far worse. When the surgery might, in fact, take their life. Dr. Pickins was in that place. He looked at me sorrowfully across the ether screen. "I don't know, man" was all he could say.

I offered, "Sandy, he's going to need a balloon if he's going to make it out of here. I don't think we have much choice." Dr. Pickins nodded. He knew it even before I said it, but he had been waiting, hoping we might somehow avoid it.

"Balloon," he announced. The "balloon pump," as it was called, (or more formally "intra-aortic balloon pump," or IABP) was an ingenious device with an inflatable balloon positioned in the aorta where it turned downward in the chest towards the abdomen. When the heart contracted, the balloon was timed to rapidly deflate, reducing the resistance the heart had to pump against. Then, while the heart rested and filled between beats, it rapidly inflated, pushing blood back to the coronary vessels supplying nourishment to the heart muscle. We used it when the heart still struggled despite high doses of medications. As Dr. Pickins threaded the assist device through the femoral artery in the patient's groin up to the descending aorta in the chest, I confirmed the correct position with my echo probe.

As we worked, I thought again about my interaction several hours earlier. This patient's whole church was praying for him. Evidently my prayers in the early morning were meant specifically for him as well. I thought, this just isn't supposed to happen.

We tried again to fill the heart with blood. The echo image on my monitor screen showed "global hypokinesis," a situation where the entire heart was contacting poorly. But we had done all we could. I nudged Dr. Pickins. "Shall we give it a try?"

"OK, let's come off slowly," he said, taking command. The OR was totally quiet as we all held our collective breaths. Right away, it was clear that Mr. Phillips' heart, even with all the drugs and balloon pump assist, was functioning just barely enough to get him off the bypass machine. Somehow, his heart had been gravely injured during the revascularization process. Neither of us knew how that had happened, but it hardly mattered. All we could do was treat him as best we could and try to get him out of the OR alive. Lela and I increased the infusion rates of the drugs we were giving, but it was like a jockey coming down the home stretch, whipping a horse that was totally out of gas.

Fifteen minutes after coming off, we were flying steady but low, like an airplane skimming the treetops. When we gave a medication to reverse the anticoagulation that had allowed Mr. Phillips to be placed on the bypass machine, his blood pressure dipped precariously. "Oh, man!" Dr. Pickins exclaimed.

"Whoa, baby. Come back now," I replied. A dose of calcium chloride stabilized the blood pressure, but just barely.

Dr. Pickins lightly touched the heart as it beat, first in one area, then another, as if caressing it might bring it back to life. He looked up at the ceiling, and I wondered if he was seeking some kind of divine help. Then he looked back down, staring at the heart, slowly shaking his head. As he attended to visible bleeding points in the chest cavity, he murmured softly, "I just don't know. Just don't know."

Over the next hour, as Dr. Pickins closed the chest, Mr. Phillips clung to life, walking a tight rope between the profound cardiac failure he was experiencing and death. The footing was precarious, with only the balloon pump and the medications we were giving allowing him to hang on. But as we prepared to move him to the ICU, he seemed to rally just a bit, as his blood pressure came up from the mid-80s to the low 90s. Not out of the woods, but better, I thought.

We got him to the ICU with his blood pressure holding steady. Despite whatever had gone wrong, it looked like he was slowly recovering. Thank God, I thought. When I left his room, I recalled my discussion with the patient yet again, and it really disturbed me. It was one thing to pray in the parking lot for a nameless patient, but quite another to have personally given him that reassurance and then see it all go so wrong. And in an ill-defined way, his entire church praying for him further distressed me. But I didn't have much time to linger with those thoughts—I had another cardiac case to get ready for surgery.

As I headed back to the OR, I passed Dr. Pickins at the nurses' station. He had one elbow perched on the desktop and his chin rested in the palm of his hand. He was staring out, looking defeated. I thought, "He has to be wondering how on earth could he have injured his patient as gravely as he did?" The fact that he had done everything according to standard operating protocols for a cardiac bypass operation would have offered scant comfort.

Following that second case, I stopped in the ICU to check on Mr. Phillips.

"How's he doing?" I asked the nurse taking care of him.

"About the same. Cardiac index around 2. His drips are maxed out and the balloon is 1 to 1. When it misreads the ECG trace and pauses, he really takes a dive. It's going to be a long night."

I drove home fast, agitated. When I walked in, I was short with Joyce, saying stupid things. I should have told her about Mr. Phillips, about my conversation with him, and then the difficulty keeping him alive, but I didn't. Instead, I fretted and pouted until I went to bed. Just before I crawled in, I knelt and said a brief prayer for Mr. Phillips.

The next day, and on the days that followed, I included Mr. Phillips in my morning ritual before entering the hospital. Each day, before heading home, I stopped in the ICU to check on him. Each day, he lingered, not any better, but not much worse. Each day, I sought out his family and discussed how he was doing. They looked exhausted, with the usual mix of fear and anticipation you see in the eyes of a family with a close relative fighting for life. They reassured me that he would somehow rally and walk out of the hospital. I wasn't so sure, but I wasn't ready to admit it.

Even though I bumped in to Dr. Pickins often the next week, neither of us brought up Mr. Phillips. I suppose it was too painful for either of us to mention him.

At around day 5 post-op he took a downhill turn, with a sharp drop in urine output. Dialysis was started on day seven. The combination of respiratory failure—he was still on a ventilator—and kidney failure, along with his barely functioning heart, put Mr. Phillips at a high likelihood of death in the hospital.

Still, I held out hope.

And each day, I prayed for him.

Around a week and a half after his operation, I went to the ICU before starting my day. When I entered Mr. Phillips' room, it was empty. I scrambled to the nurse's station and asked, fearfully, "Where is Mr. Phillips?"

One of the nurses looked up and nonchalantly answered, "Oh, he died last night. Right around 11 pm at change of shift."

It hit me hard. I reeled, having to steady myself at the counter. I was angry. Angry with Mr. Phillips for dying and angry with God for allowing him to die. But almost immediately, I was angry with myself. I silently swore. How stupid could you be? How could you possibly not have seen this coming? Did you think he was going to just miraculously recover and live another forty years? Part of me realized how much I had been in denial since his operation. Of course, he died. Once his kidneys had given out, he never had a chance, really. But a separate part of me asked, "God, didn't we have a deal, or at least kind of an understanding? What about all those prayers?"

Looking back, I suppose the only saving grace in Mr. Pickins' death was that the suffering he went through after his operation—the pain of surgery, the discomfort of a breathing tube, the misery of seeing his family's bedside vigil day after day, his total helplessness lying in that ICU bed—had ended. But I sure couldn't see any grace on the morning I learned he had died.

I asked about the family. I wondered if they felt somehow deceived, with that whole church praying, or somehow cheated, as I did. The nurse informed me, bluntly, "They left the hospital shortly after he passed." In a way, I was relieved. I'm not sure what we would have said to each other had they still been there.

I hurried off to begin my day, slightly dazed.

In the weeks that followed, I continued my daily protocol of praying, but I began to question why I was doing it. And how I was doing it. I had to admit that most of my purpose before I met Mr. Phillips had been to ask for favorable outcomes. It had been as though I was in some kind of divine cafeteria line, taking whatever I needed on my plate that day. I had thought of God as my own Cosmic Concierge, just waiting to fulfill my wishes. How foolish. The old adage that "you make your plans, and then God laughs" applies just as much to medicine as it does to ordinary life.

Over time, I accepted the limits of what I might expect from prayer. My invocations changed to a kind acknowledgment of how little control I had over things, that there were far greater forces at work. As much as I wanted to be on the Results Committee, like everyone else, I would be limited to the Work Detail. I gradually came to modifying my prayers, to asking only that my mind and hands be guided in the way that was most beneficial for my patients, that I would be able to do my part properly. And I would ask for the ability to accept whatever outcome would occur. In the end, I guess they became prayers for me as much as for my patients. After I adjusted my expectations, I still found it a process that sustained and enriched my life. It was mystical yet comforting, uncertain yet reassuring.

There has been little formal research on the effect of prayer on medical outcomes. While a few studies suggest that patients might benefit, the evidence is thin. But there have been a large number of scientific reports on such things as yoga and general "spirituality" that show psychological benefits with a diverse array of conditions. Regardless of tangible results, prayer does allow a person to acknowledge what is sacred in their life and to connect with it on a deeper level.

I've never been faced with needing the kind of surgery where my life might be in danger. If that time comes, I suppose I will silently pray for those taking care of me to do their jobs well. I know Joyce will say something to them like, "We have all been praying for David." I won't expect any kind of response like I gave while in practice. Still, even knowing the limits of prayer, it will be comforting if my doctor turns to me and says, in return, "I've already prayed for you today."

Chapter 8

FRAGILITY

WHILE A DOCTOR'S ABILITY to quickly recognize that a patient is in a crisis, then act decisively, factors into whether the patient lives or dies, it is not always determinant. Ask any seasoned physician whose practice includes critically ill patients what tips the balance to success or failure, and for many situations they will say they simply don't know. It seems that some critical situations are so tenuous, so fragile, that it's difficult to sort out what's attributed to good medical practice and what's credited to chance. There are so many intersecting influences that, in the end, all doctors can do is perform to the best of their abilities and then let the chips fall where they may. Appreciating they only control some of the variables that determine outcome makes physicians especially grateful when the sickest patients somehow survive a life-threatening calamity.

Many years into my practice, I was assigned to care for Mr. Casey, who was scheduled for a total hip replacement in OR 16. He was 75 years old and overweight, but not by much. There was a sparkle in his eyes that showed he still possessed the love of life that had given him forty years of marriage and a bunch of grandchildren. He was a "good old boy" from Tennessee who could have stepped right out from a commercial on TV, smiling with his wife on the couch because that reverse mortgage had worked out so well. When I told him we would do a spinal anesthetic, he responded the way most patients did, with, "Whatever you say, doc."

Laura Price was the CRNA working with me that day. CRNAs are nurses who take additional training in administering anesthesia, usually for three years (a third group of very qualified individuals licensed to provide anesthesia under the supervision of an anesthesiologist in around twenty states in the U.S. are called Certified Anesthesia Assistants, or CAAs). Most CRNAs work with anesthesiologists in what is termed the care team, while in some states they're allowed to practice independently. In the care team model, which was how I worked for my entire career, I was charged with evaluating patients pre-operatively, planning the anesthetic, and then supervising the CRNAs as they performed the actual hands-on care. I was there for the induction of anesthesia, during the most demanding parts of an anesthetic, and then when the patients awakened.

Although CRNAs have less training in anesthesia than anesthesiologists and lack the medical school instruction that MDs receive, they are highly educated professionals. The CRNAs I worked with in my practice were superb. But even with their considerable skills, CRNAs occasionally need to call for help from a physician. Don't be misled or anxious if anyone ever warns you that "just a nurse" will be taking care of you in the OR with the MD as backup. That is how all the anesthetics were given when I or anyone in my family needed surgery. I knew that if things ever fell apart in a case, there was nothing better than having two brains and two sets of expert hands at the head of the operating table.

Laura was a relatively new hire, having graduated from our local CRNA school less than a year earlier. While she lacked on-the-job experience, she seemed well trained and conscientious.

After Laura brought Mr. Casey into OR 16, she called me to the room to put in the spinal anesthetic. All the operating personnel were present, and it reminded me of one of the reasons working in surgery was so enjoyable—I almost always loved the people I worked with. The surgeon was Dr. Joe Slaughter, an orthopedist who I'd worked with for over fifteen years. We had a friendship outside the hospital as well. Working with Joe was easy and natural, like putting my hand into a glove. Joe was physically imposing, as many orthopedists are, standing over 6 feet tall and weighing well over 200 pounds. He looked like he might have been a lineman on his college football team back in Canada where he grew up.

Some complex surgeries required more than one surgeon to assist the chief operator, but in most cases a specially trained surgical assistant was present to help. For Mr. Casey, surgical assistant Pat Yanik would be helping Joe. Pat had been an engineer in his previous profession, so he was super qualified to assist in complex orthopedic work. Our surgical scrub nurse, the person who would hand instruments to Dr. Slaughter and who'd take them back after they'd been used, was Josephine Dowling. Josephine also would load sutures, hand Dr. Slaughter a suction catheter when needed, and provide anything else that was required to be sterile. Josephine was assigned to be Joe's scrub nurse whenever possible, since working together frequently made the handling of instruments seamless. Dr. Slaughter, Pat, and Josephine would all be "scrubbed in for the case," dressed in sterile gowns, sterile gloves, and masks.

Finally, for each operation there is a circulating nurse, whose job was to "circulate" around the room, open requested sterile equipment for the scrub nurse, document what was going on, run to the blood bank if needed, send blood samples for laboratory work, update the patient's family on how surgery was progressing, and so forth.

Whenever I did an anesthetic alone and needed something, I was totally dependent on the circulating nurse to get it for me. Betty Jack, our nurse on the case, was nearing retirement, having worked in ORs for over forty years. Even though her "rank" was a RN, she took no grief from MDs who she felt got out of hand. They were working in "her" Operating Room, and they had better behave that way. That applied to the anesthesia personnel, as well. Who couldn't love her?

I loved the concept that I was part of a team working together in the OR, with each person filling a specific position. Decades ago, the surgeon was considered "Captain of the ship," with all the others serving under his or her command. Nowadays, it's recognized that that hierarchy was unhealthy and could lead to disastrous outcomes, so each person works autonomously, with the understanding that we all work to help each other. One change that I find amazing as a culture of safety has gradually replaced that of surgeon dominance, is that in every OR in the U.S. it is accepted that at any time, any person present in the OR has the authority to stop an operation from proceeding if they feel an unrecognized danger is present, until that danger is addressed.

I most enjoyed working with operating teams where the personnel came together repeatedly, day after day, like players on a baseball team participating in games over and over as the season progressed. Those ORs ran like a well-oiled machine. However, I also could be teamed with four or more total strangers coming to work together for the first time for a complex operation, and we still generally functioned well. In that regard, I found working in the OR similar to the way recordings are made in Nashville. A producer assembles whatever musicians are felt necessary, and even though they have never worked together before or even heard the rudimentary demo recording of what they'll be working on, within minutes they're producing beautiful music.

I witnessed every kind of atmosphere imaginable in the OR, though it usually followed the seriousness of the operation or the personality of the surgeon. There is an unwritten understanding that the music that is played—if music is played at all—is chosen by the surgeon, presumably to let that individual work in an environment he or she finds most comfortable.

Once our monitors were in place, we placed Mr. Casey on his side and had him curl up, with his knees tucked up to his chest. Betty had opened up the spinal anesthesia tray as well as my sterile gloves, and I slipped them on. I prepped his lower back with an antiseptic and then applied a sterile drape. I pushed against the bones in the midline of his back and identified the space between two bony prominences where I would enter the skin. After injecting some local anesthetic, I inserted a long thin needle to a depth of around an inch and half and had no trouble entering the CSF where the anesthetic would be given, feeling a distinct "pop, pop" as it moved through the two deepest tissue layers that surrounded it. I removed the inner stylette from the needle, and within a few seconds I saw fluid emerge from its end, drip . . . drip. I felt a rush. No matter how many spinal anesthetics I gave, I never lost the wonder I felt when I saw CSF for the first time during medical school. The liquid is clear, crystal clear, almost shining in its translucence. There is no liquid more beautiful than CSF, and none possesses a greater clarity. I could envision a pool of CSF fifty feet deep, and I would expect to see objects on the bottom as clearly as if they were floating on top.

I attached a syringe to the needle and injected the local anesthetic that would keep Mr. Casey numb from the waist down for the next two hours. I then pulled out the needle.

Once we got Mr. Casey positioned for surgery, lying on his side with the bad hip up, Laura started an infusion of propofol to sedate him and spare him the sounds of his surgery. Many anesthetists refer to propofol as "mother's milk," because it's a white liquid. You may have heard of it as "the Michael Jackson medicine," but in the hands of anesthetists, it's an extremely predictable and safe anesthetic. In lower doses, propofol gently puts patients into a light state of sedation, blissful and mellow. With larger doses, a light sleep comes, and with still more, you get a general anesthetic. So, you had to be careful how much you gave.

In addition to his bad hip, Mr. Casey had obstructive sleep apnea, or OSA, a condition that made sedating him a bit more hazardous. OSA causes varying degrees of upper airway obstruction when patients fall asleep, and the deeper the sleep the greater the obstruction. But Laura would observe his respirations breath by breath, monitoring his oxygenation with a pulse oximeter, and adjusting the dose of propofol accordingly. If he got into trouble, she could recognize and correct it pretty quickly or call me for help.

Once we got Mr. Casey sleepy and the surgical prep was underway, I left the room, telling Laura, "Give a call if you need me."

About an hour into the operation, I heard the overhead operating room speaker system announce, "Dr. Alfery, room 16." There was no urgency in the request, but since I happened to be right outside that OR, I entered within around ten seconds. Immediately, I saw that Laura was struggling, trying to hold a facemask on Mr. Casey. Needing a facemask was alarming, indicating that he was not breathing well enough on his own. As I strode across the room, I didn't see an end-tidal carbon dioxide trace on the monitor. Carbon dioxide was one of the gasses that exited the lungs when a patient breathed, so its absence from the exhaled gas being sampled indicated that either there was no effective breathing or that the facemask was being applied so poorly that the monitor was not picking it up. Additionally, Mr. Casey's face looked bluish in color. The pulse oximeter that should have been displaying the actual oxygen level in his blood had been knocked off, so its trace was absent from the monitor screen as well.

"Call a code," I barked out, ordering the distress call would be sent throughout the entire operating theater, asking for any available help to rush to OR 16 to assist with our crisis (unlike "codes" that occur anywhere else in the hospital, those that occur in an OR are managed only by individuals working in the operating theater).

By the time I reached the head of the operating table, my heart was already beginning to pound. I pressed my fingers hard on Mr. Casey's neck to feel for a carotid pulse. Nothing. That meant no effective blood flow to the body, cause as yet to be determined. With the patient in this much trouble, there was no way we could properly take care him on his side. I said to the surgeon, "Joe, we need to turn this guy flat onto his back, right now."

Quickly turning the patient with a gaping open wound over his hip would be a challenge. Dr. Slaughter didn't hesitate. "Towel clips," he snarled. "I need a bunch," and they quickly appeared in his hand. With the help of his assistant, Pat, who pulled the incision edges together, Joe pierced the edges of both sides with hooked fasteners that normally held green surgical towels in place, to fashion an improvised wound closure. He used four or five clips, placed in rapid succession—chick, chick, chick—and then Pat seamlessly covered the area with a sterile towel. In less than thirty seconds you heard, "One, two, three," and Mr. Casey was pulled to the far edge of the operating table and then rolled flat onto his back.

"Start compressions," I said, indicating that we were going straight to CPR. Pat began pumping, leaning over with two hands folded on mid-chest, pushing deeply down at a rate of around a hundred times per minute.

I took the facemask from Laura and attempted to get oxygen into Mr. Casey. Nothing. I grabbed a laryngoscope and an ETT and said, "Stop pumping for a second." Pat immediately ceased, and I easily passed the tube into the trachea. I listened quickly for breath sounds to make sure it was in the right place, and then I felt for the carotid pulse again. Nothing. "Start compressions," I repeated, and Pat resumed. "One, two, three . . . ."

Oh God, this is bad, I thought.

Within a few seconds of my calling the code, one of my physician partners burst into the room along with two spare CRNAs. Additional nurses streamed in with the "code cart," a rolling, red Sears Craftsman tool chest carrying a defibrillator in case the heart needed shocking, as well as drawers filled with drugs. The other name for a code cart was a "crash cart," presumably because it was used for patients whose condition had crashed, like an airplane suddenly plummeting to the ground.

It seemed as if everyone in the room was talking at once, each stating what he or she was doing or needed to do. That happens early in most codes, where there is a lot of excitement and so much noise that it's difficult to hear what the person running the resuscitation needs. I spoke loudly, "Please don't talk unless it's necessary." The room fell silent except for Pat's grunting, "One, two, three . . . " as he leaned into Mr. Casey's chest.

I looked up at the anesthesia monitor and saw a sinus rhythm, a normal complex of the electrical activity of the heart, but the heart itself was not pumping vigorously enough to provide a pulse I could feel. The term for that is EMD, or electromechanical dissociation, and it is invariably fatal if you can't find the cause and fix it. "A milligram of epi, please," I said, directing that we give one milligram of the drug epinephrine in order to stimulate cardiac contractions. Also known as adrenaline, this is the hormone suddenly released into your blood when a child runs out into the street, you slam on your brakes, and ten seconds later your heart is banging in your chest.

A nurse manning the code cart pulled the medication out and repeated, "One milligram epinephrine." It was easy to misinterpret or miss-hear what was asked for, especially when an abbreviated name was used, so to avoid giving a similar sounding but incorrect drug in a crisis situation, the drug names are always repeated before being administered.

Another nurse hooked up the defibrillator with its three leads, and its monitor screen confirmed the rhythm was sinus. I had a quick discussion with a second partner who'd arrived, trying to keep my voice calm and steady, to not reveal the fright I was feeling. "Got called to the room, cyanotic, totally crapped out. Turned him flat, tubed him, CPR, sinus but no pulse. One milligram of epi in. Not sure what's going on."

After a minute of additional CPR and allowing the epinephrine to take effect, I directed, "Stop pumping." I felt again for a pulse in the neck. "I'm not sure if I feel one or not," I stated. "Can you check the groin?"

Joe and Pat simultaneously felt for a femoral pulse, and one of them reported, "I think I've got a weak one."

"Keep pumping," I responded. "Another milligram of epi, please." A minute later there was a definite pulsation that I could feel, and relieved, I said, "Stop pumping. We've got a good one now."

Conversation returned among the nurses and techs, a kind of murmuring background noise discussing the emergency they'd just witnessed. Responders slowly drifted out of the room.

As they exited, Laura quietly told me she'd struggled with the airway and Mr. Casey's breathing for a considerable time before Dr. Slaughter had looked over the ether screen and asked, diplomatically, "Why don't we get Dr. Alfery in here?" I felt a wave of nausea. It was Laura's responsibility to know when to call for assistance, and she hadn't. For Joe to see her flounder to the point he needed to suggest I be summoned meant I was called far later than I should have been. And with Mr. Casey in such obvious distress, the call should have been STAT. I couldn't help but wonder if our resuscitation had been started too late, if some permanent damage due to lack of oxygen to the brain might have resulted from the delay. Still, we had jumped on the situation just as soon as I had arrived, and the code had gone as smoothly as I could have hoped. In any event, I couldn't worry about that now.

Mr. Casey's pulse remained strong, and one of my partners slipped an intravenous cannula into the radial artery in his wrist; from that we drew blood for a bedside analysis of his blood gases. That would tell us how well he was oxygenating. In addition, it would show if there was any buildup of acid in his blood, indicating that there had been inadequate perfusion to his tissues during the crisis. I stared at the screen of the analyzer, as if that might force it to display the results faster. Within a minute it appeared and showed there was, in fact, a modest build up, but not an alarming amount. That much, at least, was reassuring.

I called for a transesophageal echocardiogram probe and slid it into Mr. Casey's esophagus in order to actually look at an image of his heart beating on a monitor screen. Visualizing the heart might give us insight into why the organ had pumped so poorly that Mr. Casey required CPR. Had it been caused by a primary cardiac problem or by a breathing problem? Maybe a fat embolus to the heart, as was known to occur in total hip replacements? The image that appeared showed his heart was pumping normally, even extra vigorously, due to the residual effects of the epinephrine. So, no apparent damage there, but also no fat embolus and cardiac cause for his collapse, as it would have not yet fully recovered. It had to be a respiratory reason. I wondered again if the delay in recognizing it had caused any permanent damage, or if this would turn out to be simply a scary near miss.

Overall, I was grateful that we got Mr. Casey stable within ten minutes. Within another forty minutes, Dr. Slaughter had the operation completed. All I needed to do was to turn off the anesthetic gas that we had started once the resuscitation was successful, and Mr. Casey would awaken. But he didn't. Even after the gas had been off for a full twenty minutes, there was no sign of consciousness. My head started to spin as I considered the trouble we were in. I administered several doses of naloxone and flumazenil, drugs that would reverse the effects of the intravenous narcotics and sedatives that had been given early in the anesthetic, in hopes that they were keeping Mr. Casey asleep, but I knew that was a long shot.

We waited.

There was still no sign of consciousness after forty minutes. I pinched the skin above his collarbone, hard. Nothing. I wiggled the ETT in and out, an intense stimulation that would cause coughing even in a patient under a modest stage of anesthesia. Still nothing. That was just so, so bad. I felt sick to my stomach, as if I might throw up. I took a deep breath, and the feeling lessened. Surely some brain damage had occurred. How much, I wondered? Would he ever awaken? And if he did, how impaired would he be?

I announced to the circulating nurse, "We need an ICU bed." I turned to leave to go talk with the family. Laura would continue to look after Mr.

Casey until we got him to the ICU. Her face was white as I headed for the door. Pat had hung around to see how Mr. Casey would wake up, and he was still there as I reached the door to the OR. As I opened it, he remarked, "Dr. Alfery, if I ever have to be in a code, I want you to run it. That was so well done." He was nice to say that, but it was scant comfort. I wondered if he was just trying to make me feel better. I thanked him and left quickly.

I went down to the waiting area on the first floor and asked one of the nurses to call for Mr. Casey's family. It was going to be a tough conversation. I considered how much detail to provide, not even sure myself of the exact timing of events prior to being called to the OR. I had a duty to be truthful with the family. But what was the actual truth? Sure, I could have been called earlier, so things hadn't been done perfectly, but medicine was an imperfect science. Were we negligent if Mr. Casey suffered permanent damage? As practitioners, Laura and I were required to meet the standard of care. In legal terms, that was defined as the level of care that a prudent practitioner with the same training and experience would provide in a similar set of circumstances in our community. Specifically, it didn't call for the absolute *best* possible care to be delivered. I thought we met the criteria, but I wasn't certain. I tried to balance giving enough factual information to convey the gist of what had occurred, but not so much that they would question the care we gave. No reason to put my thumb on the judgment scale with an interpretation that might not even be warranted. That could come later, if need be.

Mr. Casey's wife appeared, along with one of her adult daughters. They were ushered into a consultation room where we sat down together. I put on a serious face, though not too serious. I described the events in the OR, but I omitted that Dr. Slaughter had to ask that I be called. "With the spinal anesthetic, Mr. Casey had some difficulty breathing during surgery, and we tried to assist him, but we were unable to do that adequately, so we needed to insert a breathing tube. The poor breathing affected his heart so much that we had to do CPR and give some powerful drugs to get it back pumping properly. At this point, his heart is doing fine, but he has not awakened. That is very worrisome. It is possible that he had some brain damage from our struggles, but we can't say for sure."

I paused in my discussion. The mother and daughter looked at each other and then back at me. They looked dazed, like two deer staring into headlights.

I continued. "We are going to bring him up to the ICU for management, and I am going to suggest a very new treatment regimen in hopes that it helps him awaken. I'm going to ask the ICU doctors to cool his body down and sedate him for a couple of days to rest his brain in hopes that it allows a full recovery when he is warmed back up and the sedation is turned off. I wish I could tell you that he will make it back to the Mr. Casey who went into surgery, but I'm afraid I can't." I paused again. Mother and daughter looked again at each other, and they gripped each other's hands. They turned back to me.

"We are going to give him every possible chance to return to the Mr. Casey who went in for surgery this morning. I will stay in contact with you over the next days to let you know how we are doing. I'm sorry to give you this news, and I know it's a shock. I wish I could be more specific about his chances for a full recovery, but I simply can't. We will just hope and pray for a full return to normal." I tried to balance my words, to fall in between the gravity of the situation and my wish for recovery. I really didn't know how much hope we should have, and I suppose I said what I had as much for me as for the family.

They'd listened in silence, looking stunned. I knew they would only comprehend some of what I said, that it was simply too much to take in at once. Mr. Casey's wife had a few general questions about how the next couple of days might go, but the daughter remained silent. As I turned to leave, they both expressed their gratitude for me getting Mr. Casey's heart going after it had failed. I felt like a fraud accepting it.

I went back up to the OR and called Dr. Francis Bannon, the ICU doctor on duty that day who would assume Mr. Casey's care.

"Hey, Francis," I began. "David Alfery here. I've got a guy in the OR for a total hip that arrested. We got him back, but he's still on the ventilator. He's going to be up there in around twenty minutes, and I wanted to give you a heads up and some details."

"Right. How's he doing now? Responding?"

"Afraid not. Woke up dead."

"What?" Evidently Francis had never heard that expression before, and looking back, I think very few doctors who worked outside of surgery used it. It was a phrase that the neurosurgeons sometimes spoke after a craniotomy, a sardonic expression that avoided describing the crushing reality that their patient might die despite a surgery that had seemingly gone well.

I immediately regretted my comment, realizing that my response had been inappropriate. I explained, "He hasn't awakened from his anesthesia, and it's been off for an hour now. I'm obviously very worried about his brain. I think we ought to cool him down for a couple of days. I don't think we have anything to lose."

My suggestion for using therapeutic hypothermia, as it was then called, was based on Guidelines by the American Heart Association that had been published just a year earlier. They recommended that patients suffering a cardiac arrest outside the hospital who did not awaken after resuscitation when they got to the hospital be sedated and deliberately cooled to around 32 degrees Centigrade (89.6 degrees Fahrenheit) for several days to increase their chance of making a full neurologic recovery. The cooling therapy was so new it had never been described in the anesthesia literature, so to my knowledge, Mr. Casey would be the first one done in this setting in the world.

Francis paused for a moment. "I don't think the American Heart Guidelines apply to this situation. Maybe we should wait a couple hours to see if he wakes up."

I came back quickly, desperately. "Francis, we've got nothing to lose. Let's cool him now," I pleaded. He relented.

Later that afternoon, I went to the ICU to see Mr. Casey. A cooling blanket was draped over him, and his rectal temperature readout on the monitor reflected how his body temperature had fallen. A propofol infusion was running, providing sedation. He would be kept this way for the next two days and then allowed to rewarm and ideally awaken on the third day. (You have undoubtedly heard the term "medically induced coma" for patients on mechanical ventilators. Actually, that term almost always refers to patients who are kept in a light state of sleep—usually by infusions of a sedative along with a narcotic—while the machine is breathing for them. Unfortunately, Mr. Casey was already in a true coma when his propofol infusion was started. The drug would lower the metabolic needs of his brain in hopes of getting an optimal recovery of its function, as evidenced by his ability to fully "awaken" when the infusion was discontinued)

I went to the ICU waiting room and brought Mrs. Casey up to date. I repeated how we couldn't know if Mr. Casey would awaken after the therapy was finished, and if he did, what kind of shape he would be in. I told her I was praying for a full recovery. She looked at me with trust in her eyes and thanked me again for the care we were providing.

Before going home, I found Laura, and we sat down for a debriefing of the events in the OR. She told me she had struggled with Mr. Casey's airway for a prolonged period, several minutes at least. She thought she was handling it adequately, or at least she kept telling herself that. It had taken Dr. Slaughter to recognize that she wasn't. I told her that when things looked bad, she had to trust they were at least as bad as they seemed. If there was even a trace of doubt in her mind that her therapy was ineffective, she should call me, and call quickly. Laura was a good CRNA, and she understood. Like so many things in medicine, it would take a bad experience for the lesson to sink in.

I went home and walked in the house without speaking. Joyce always had a way of knowing when something upsetting had happened. She put her arms around me and then stood back and looked me in the eye. "Do you want to talk about it?"

I didn't answer. I went to a cabinet and pulled out a bottle of scotch. I put one huge square cube of ice in a glass and covered it with a couple of shots. I tilted some back into my throat before it could even chill. The burn I felt as I swallowed it seemed fitting for what was going on in my mind.

Joyce came up to me and wrapped her arms around me, but she now said nothing. Usually, I kept events like I'd experienced with Mr. Casey to myself, nursing my inner wounds in private, but not this time. I blurted out the entire episode in one lengthy run-on sentence, from the moment I was called to Mr. Casey's room to the time I spent with Mrs. Casey, telling her the truth, but not the whole truth. It was as much confession as it was explanation.

Given Joyce's training as a nurse, she understood the issues and the pressure I felt. She tried to reassure me, but it didn't help. She let me go and I left the room. I sulked and stewed the rest of the evening. I thought about Mr. Casey constantly until I went to bed. When I awoke, he was the first thing on my mind.

For the next two days, I went to see Mr. Casey when I got to the hospital in the morning and again before I went home. Each time, as I entered his room, I looked for any sign that he was recovering, any response to stimulation or movement. Given that he remained in an artificial state of hibernation and sedation, this was completely unrealistic. But still I checked, asking his nurse each time, "Any response? Anything? Anything at all?" Nothing.

During the two days of treatment, I was in agony, but I knew it was far worse for his family. With each visit I sought out Mrs. Casey and gave her the progress report that there really wasn't any progress to report.

On the third day after the arrest, I knew the propofol infusion would be stopped and Mr. Casey warmed back up to a normal temperature. I was busy in the OR in the morning, so I couldn't get to the ICU until midafternoon. When I arrived, I cautiously slipped into his room. Yes! There he was, breathing tube still in place, but his twinkling eyes were open, and his arms were moving about. He had awakened and was responding appropriately, even writing notes with a marker on a white board! My heart soared. I felt the weight of the world lift off my shoulders.

I leaned over and said, "Mr. Casey, Dr. Alfery here, your anesthesiologist. I know you can't talk, but we'll get that breathing tube out just as soon as we can. You had a little breathing problem in the Operating Room we had to take care of, but you're actually doing fine now." I went to find Mrs. Casey, and she told me she had seen him in the morning, already awakening. She wrapped her arms around me and thanked me yet again.

I ran back down to the OR and had Laura relieved from her case for a short break. I relayed the news of Mr. Casey's recovery, and when I got to the part where I said, "fully responsive," she gasped and hugged me tightly. We jumped up and down together, giggling like school children. It was as though we'd just heard from the Governor: sentence commuted, execution stayed!

Mr. Casey had the ETT removed later that afternoon. The next day, after he moved out of the ICU, I went to see him in his room on the ward. I reminded him who I was, and he simply asked, "Doc, what happened?" As I had with his wife, I gave him a slightly sanitized explanation, emphasizing most of all how grateful we were that he'd recovered. He grabbed my hand, pumped it vigorously, and thanked me. I danced out of the room. That was the last time I ever saw him.

A couple of weeks later, I was having a quick lunch with Dr. Slaughter in the doctor's lounge. We were talking about something trivial until he said, "Hey, I saw Mr. Casey back in the office this morning. He wanted me to thank you again for saving his life."

My first thought was how close he had come to losing it. Then I thought of something else. There is an image first proposed by a man named James Reason for how a simple mistake can get by all the safety guardrails erected in medicine and cause a patient harm. It is called the Swiss cheese model, or more recently, the cumulative act effect. The model visualizes injury to a patient as an arrow traveling through the holes in a number of stacked slices of Swiss cheese, with each hole representing a failure of safety, such as ignoring a patient alarm or omitting a check list—or not quickly calling for help. When a series of failures line up precisely, the arrow travels through the holes unimpeded, and an injury results. I sometimes think there's a similar explanation for how patients can survive an episode with seemingly improbable occurrences where they should have died, but somehow, against all odds, they made it through.

I thought back to Mr. Casey. I thought of the fragility of his hospital course and how that mirrored the fragility of the patients doctors so often care for. I thought of how his outcome had been delicately balanced as if on a cliff, where a change in a single factor could have sent him careening down on the side of perishing. Even though Laura failed to call for me when she could have, Joe had looked up from the operation and noticed her struggling. Rather than assume Laura was handling it properly, he looked further and suggested I be called. Rather than reassuring Dr. Slaughter she didn't need to, Laura had complied. Even though it wasn't a STAT call, I had been right outside room 16 when it was made, and then instead of carrying on with whatever task I was going to do, I came into the room immediately. My experience allowed me to rapidly assess how desperate the situation was and call the code without delay. From there, everything had gone as smoothly as it possibly could, including the cooling. Ultimately, Mr. Casey managed to recover completely. Who knows why all his cheese slices lined up precisely to allow that arrow of recovery to slip through, while any other patient would have died? It was more than remarkable. It was a mystery of medicine, a miracle.

Albert Einstein famously said, "There are two ways to live your life. One is as though nothing is a miracle. The other is as though everything is a miracle." I know there are many who would disagree with me, but I have to think there was an element of divine intervention in Mr. Casey's recovery, and act of grace by God when he needed it most.

There were other patients I took care of like him, who beat seemingly impossible odds, but none quite as dramatic. Still, there were improbable survivors and others who unexpectedly perished. In each, if you looked carefully enough, you found a cascade of factors that tilted the scale to survival or death, where the Swiss cheese lined up just enough to provide that outcome.

Of course, we are all aware of similar circumstances in our ordinary lives, happenings that display the precariousness of our existence. The person who doesn't see the red light and speeds into the intersection, just barely zooming through the gap left by one car whose driver has momentarily sped up to make an appointment and another that has slowed just enough as the driver looked over at a billboard. Or the people we hear about for whom a series of seemingly trivial events led to their narrowly missing the flight that crashed. For those outcomes, just like Mr. Casey, we can only marvel at the good fortune.

Knowing how easily minor events could stack up to cause terrible results and how truly unpredictable were the disastrous happenings that could occur, caused a kind of background white noise of anxiety I felt during my entire practice life. A general feeling of disquiet was an unwelcome companion I could never quite get rid of. Was a crisis right around the corner, ready to hit me head on? My apprehension was greatest at night when I was on call and consciously aware of it. It was like I was somehow plugged into the electrical socket in the wall, never able to relax. I repeatedly told myself how silly it was to be nervous, that I had never faced a situation I couldn't manage, but all the logic in the world could not dispel that buzz of unease. Even in an ordinary workday, a feeling of tension often bubbled beneath the surface. Crazy as it seems, there were some days when, driving in to work, I consciously wondered, will I kill anyone today? And other days when, going home, I felt relief, thinking, you got through another day without killing a patient.

I have had many other physicians tell me they have had a similar unseen, unwelcome shadow follow them in their practice, sometimes looming large, but always at least a sliver of a realization that catastrophe could be but a moment away. There is a fair chance your own doctor has felt that, as well.

I turned to Joe and nodded. "Yeah. I'm pretty happy he pulled through." Then I turned back to finish my lunch.

Chapter 9

EXPECTATIONS

NASHVILLE TURNED OUT TO be a great place to practice medicine. During the time I lived there, it evolved from a sleepy little recording hub—"Music City USA"—to a vibrant high-tech community considered to be one of the "it" cities in the U.S. Vanderbilt University is there, attracting and churning out highly trained medical doctors, nurses, and techs. After Hospital Corporation of America was founded in the city in 1968 and made many of its executives millionaires, it became the place where, year after year, more medical start-up companies were formed and went public than anywhere else in America. As a result, by working in Nashville, I always felt I was on the cutting edge of whatever advances were being made in medicine.

As long as I kept working hard, pretty much all of my expectations could be fulfilled—a nice family, a nice house, a nice car, nice vacations. But once faith entered my life, I knew there were other dimensions it should entail, deeper things that could make it more meaningful. I looked around me and found that a number of my fellow physicians had gone on medical missions. Once they'd gone on one, they went back on others. I knew nonmedical people who'd gone on nonmedical missions, and they often returned as well. All those individuals spoke of how their view of life had been changed by their experiences. They seemed to *expect* fewer things in their life, and they were more grateful for the things they had. For the physicians, what they *didn't* have was much patience with doctors who were always complaining about how tough their life was.

Eventually, I signed up for a trip to the Caribbean with a church group and spent a week doing anesthesia for simple general surgery cases. My partner, Dr. Mick Saggio, went with me, fulfilling his own curiosity about what these missions were like. The trip was a turning point for both of us; we came back exhausted but energized. And as it had been for those other doctors, our expectations of life changed.

We went on quite a few missions together over the next ten years. Each was rewarding, but the one that affected us most was the one to Romania, where we worked for a week at the Pitesti Pediatric Hospital. This was a nine-story building that looked like it was built in the 1940s or 1950s, with one floor devoted to an orphanage. The long rooms on that floor were Spartan, consisting of a string of beds or cribs and little else. No tables, no lamps, no books, no toys. No joy. Just orphans. Food for those children was barely adequate; we were told they were given a small bowl of some kind of gruel once per day. Some of the older kids would go out from the hospital in the early morning to try to find something extra to eat. If we took a quick break between cases and looked outside around 9 o'clock, we could see a little parade of pajama-clad children heading back with loaves of yesterday's bread under their arms, given to them by kind-hearted merchants who knew how desperate their living conditions were.

The ORs were Spartan as well. Back home, I used highly automated anesthesia machines costing upwards of $50,000.00. In our Romanian operating theaters, there were no machines at all. There were, nevertheless, two tables in each room, so we would do surgery on two children at the same time. For delivering anesthesia, rather than a central oxygen supply from the hospital coming to a sophisticated machine, we had a single fat, tall, green oxygen cylinder with a hose coming out, splitting into a Y-piece and tubing that ran to two gas vaporizers. A vaporizer was the critical part of an anesthesia machine, the device that turns liquid anesthetic agent into a gas to be breathed. It was the one part of the mechanism that you could not do without, and it was the single part we had. We taped them to a table-top lest they be jarred and spill over, delivering an overdose of the agent being administered. The vaporizer led to the breathing apparatus we used with our children. When the patients exhaled, rather than their anesthetic gases being scavenged and removed from the OR as was done at home, they were just breathed out into the room. Over the course of the day, the sweet sickly smell of our vapors permeated the air, giving a kind of gentle buzz to those working.

Since we were doing orthopedic procedures on that mission trip, there were X-rays that needed examining. Having no viewing boxes, the surgeons would just tape the films to the windows to let light shine through them for a primitive inspection.

When an operation was finished, we would place our patients on an ancient stretcher to leave the OR, the wheels squeaking in time as they spun on rusted axels.

The rudimentary Post-Anesthetic Care Unit (PACU, and also called Recovery Room) was one floor above, and to get there we took an elevator commanded by a large, grey haired Romanian woman. Apparently wearing the same plain dress the entire week, she sat on a round wooden stool and pulled open a rusted metal gate that allowed entry. The gate was cross hatched with corroded metal that folded together as it opened, then spread back apart as it closed, like you might see in a detective movie from the 40s. As we entered the elevator, she would nod her head, approvingly, as if to say we had done what was needed, and now she would take us up a floor. Once inside, she scraped the gate closed, moved a large dial to the number of the next floor, and then pushed a lever to its side. The elevator would groan as it began its slow ascent, rumbling deeply as it inched upwards, shaking and rattling along the way. The elevator operator would jabber excitedly in Romanian to the women gathered in the hallway of the floor of the PACU when we arrived, announcing who was our patient. The only word I could understand was the name of the child we had operated on. With each arrival, news rapidly spread down the hallway, each woman repeating what she had been told, like a telegraph message moving from pole to pole.

One day between operations, an emergency call was put out for an anesthesiologist. I was the only one available, so a nurse quickly escorted me to the Emergency Room (ER). On my way, I was told that a little Gypsy boy had been run over by a bus. Whisked into the ER, I saw none of the usual equipment one would find back home. No monitors. No automatic blood pressure devises. No oxygen regulators on the wall. No suctions machines. Instead, I found two individuals leaning over, sewing up a large gash on the boy's leg. I moved to the head of his stretcher and looked down at a child about seven years old. He looked lifeless, deep blue in color, almost black. I reached down and felt a strong pulse in his neck, and perhaps my stirring him caused him to take a shallow breath.

"Ambu bag, please, and oxygen," I said. I took over his breathing with the bag, and the bluish color lessened as I got oxygen into his lungs. When I asked for vital signs, a nurse in a crisp white dress stepped forward and took a blood pressure by pumping up a cuff, the way we did years ago back home. As there was no ECG monitor, another nurse counted a pulse as she checked her wristwatch. The pressure was alarmingly high and the heart rate slow. Both were ominous signs, consistent with dangerously elevated pressure within the boy's head from his accident.

Within a few minutes, the boy was back to a normal pink color, and I took a closer look. His shirt was torn and dirty. Gravel covered his chin and was imbedded in a deep laceration that went all the way through his lower lip. I thought, briefly, it's going to hurt like hell to wash that out. And then, I thought—if he lives that long. Blood had trickled like a little stream from the corner of his mouth, now dried up as a brown dried scab on his cheek. More blood had pooled and dried on the sheet on which he lay. Still more blood snaked its way out of an ear canal and dried in a puddle on his neck. The rest of his face was smooth, unblemished. I pulled open his eyelids. His pupils were widely dilated, dying eyes that stared out vacantly. Another ominous sign.

"I need a laryngoscope and a five and a half endotracheal tube" was my second request. Someone quickly handed them to me. ETTs came in a wide variety of sizes, ranging all the way from those used in tiny pre-term infants that looked like a cocktail straw, to others the size of a garden hose, suitable for large men. As an anesthesiologist whose practice consisted almost entirely of adult patients, I had to guess at the correct size for the boy. There were formulas the non-pediatric guys like me used to determine the proper size, such as 4 plus the age of a child divided by 4, but I didn't really know how old the boy was. If I picked one too large, I could damage the trachea. Too small would have a big leak. In the end, the ETT had to "feel" right as you placed it. Fortunately, I guessed right, as the size five and a half slid into his trachea without difficulty. Disturbingly, though, the boy made no effort to resist my securing his airway, an indication he was deeply comatose, clinging to life. It was likely his head injury would prove fatal, but we would do our best.

I asked a nurse to take over squeezing the Ambu bag so I could better examine the patient. I peered at his face again, and if innocence can have a look, he had it. He was pretty, almost feminine in appearance, with the dark features common to Gypsies—straight black hair, brown complexion, thick eyebrows for a child, dark eyes, long delicate eyelashes. But there wasn't much to him. He was rail thin and looked malnourished, and I thought he was likely short for his age. His feet were bare and dirty. I pressed my hand into his abdomen. His belly was soft, so it didn't look like there was any bleeding inside. Well, I thought, at least he had that going for him. I tried not to think of my children back home.

Because one has to be concerned that the neck might also be injured in the context of head trauma, I had to prevent any movement of his skull from a midline position until X-rays had ruled such injury out, as that could cause damage to the spinal cord. "Can I get a cervical collar?" I asked.

A nurse disappeared from the room and returned a moment later. She held a cardboard box out to me. "I'm sorry, Sir, we don't have any collars. But we have this."

I nodded. I gently placed his head on the cardboard and then encircled it with 2-inch tape. It would have to do.

The boy's only chance at survival was if there was bleeding inside the skull that could be surgically evacuated. That meant he needed the specialized imaging of a CT scan. I spoke, reluctantly, fearing the answer. "We're going to need an emergency CT scan if there's any chance of this little guy surviving."

The reply came quickly. "The only CT scan in Romania is in Bucharest."

I gave a little gasp and shook my head. I expected there would at least be one in Pitesti, with a population of 170,000. In Nashville, I bet we had more than twenty scanners, with a couple even located in strip malls. Then I wondered, if a scan indicated that surgery was needed, would there even be a neurosurgeon available for him? I paused and thought what to do. With his grievous injury and everything seemingly stacked against him, should we even proceed? But how do you give up on a child unless you know, and I mean *know for certain*, that there is no hope for survival? What if I were his father? What If I heard, well, they didn't think he would live, and even if he did, they weren't sure what kind of shape he would end up in, so they just let him die?

Bucharest was ninety miles away. I decided, "Well, let's give him 20 mg. of Lasix and get him there as soon as we can." Lasix is a drug that would temporarily reduce the swelling in his brain, but I was pretty sure he was doomed.

Within a couple of minutes, two burly young men marched into the ER, one in front holding the ends of two poles, and the other behind holding the opposite ends. In between was a blanket that was secured to the rods, hanging down as a sling. I had seen hand carried stretchers such as this before, but only in black and white photographs from World War I or II. We carefully lifted the child onto the stretcher. I took a last look at him, and it was as if I was staring at my own child. I accompanied the stretcher-bearers as they brought him outside to a waiting ambulance. I watched as the vehicle drove away, wondering how long the boy would last. I learned later that evening that he had died.

It was heart breaking. I could only wonder, might he have survived had he sustained that injury in a major American city? Though I was almost certain he was destined to perish, hearing of his death was a kind of painful relief to me. I don't know why. Maybe I just wanted to get it over with and have the tragedy end. But there is no ending with little Gypsy boys when they collide in your life the way he did. Some wrecks are so bad that, even though you fix the dents and paint the metal, the car never runs exactly the same way ever again, because one of the broken parts is irreplaceable. Even today, after more than twenty years have elapsed, I vividly recall that little boy's face.

In some ways, though, having religious faith in my life made the death of the Gypsy boy somehow more bearable. I didn't believe that God's fingerprints could be found at the scene of the crime, and I accepted that I would never understand "why bad things happen to good people." I also understood that God would not change the immutable laws of nature, that once a fatal injury had occurred, there would be no sudden miraculous cure. What was important was my response, to realize the frailty and evanescence of life, and to hold little boys like the Gypsy child dear. With that foundation, I could move away from questioning, accept what had happened, and focus my emotions on simply grieving his loss.

One other patient affected me just as much. Lidia was an 11-year-old girl who had been born with several abnormalities. Most prominently, she had a condition called syndactyly, where there is fusion of one or more fingers to the ones next to it, connected by skin tissue. Her hands resembled a seal's flipper, and she could use her fingers, but not well. Lidia had other abnormalities, and her orthopedic surgeon opted to operate on an accompanying condition called equniovarus deformity, commonly called clubfeet ("equinovarus" is one of the Latin terms doctors use, with "equino" referring to "like a horse," and "varus," translating as "turned inwards"). Lidia's feet were pointed almost straight down, nearly parallel with her lower legs, the most severe case one could imagine. She hadn't walked in years. The operation to correct this would be a "forefoot osteotomy," a brutal procedure that consisted of sawing and removing a triangular wedge of bone from the front and outside of her ankles in order to allow her feet to be bent back outwards and upwards, with her soles oriented towards the ground. Her feet would be fused in this position, fixed with large screws across the bone pieces. Repair of the syndactyly would await return of the mission team the following year, if we did return.

Brought into the OR by wheelchair, alone, Lidia hopped up onto the operating table eagerly and lay back, chirping out, "Good morning," as she did so. Like most of the children we took care of that week, she spoke English surprisingly well. With her arms at her sides, she looked straight up at me, smiled broadly, and seemed almost giddy. I took her left forearm and wrapped a thin rubber tourniquet around it in order to start an IV. When I held her hand to stretch out a vein, her syndactyly was obvious, the thin webbing of skin extending halfway to each fingertip. She did not seem self-conscious about it, though. I slipped the IV catheter in easily, and she did not flinch. As I applied my blood pressure cuff and ECG pads, I could see her feet protruding from the sheet covering her body, pointing almost in line with her lower legs.

I picked up my anesthesia facemask to give her oxygen, but I paused, gazing down at the look of sweet serenity on her face. She licked her lips and smiled up at me, expectantly, approvingly. As the induction medications flowed into her vein and she drifted off to sleep, I wondered—what she was thinking? What was she expecting? Maybe she would be happy to be able to walk again, albeit with difficulty, but would she ever get her other physical problems fixed?

The surgeon had elected to repair both feet in this one procedure. Given that there was no certainty he would ever be back to the Pitesti Children's Hospital, the postoperative care would be done by Romanian hospital staff. The operative team would have long departed when her casts were removed in around a week's time.

The orthopedic work proceeded smoothly, efficiently. When you watched one of these operations, there was nothing elegant about it. An electric saw was used to cut through the bones in the ankle, and it squealed out a high-pitched screech as it did so. As soon as the blade was withdrawn from a bone, it was free of resistance, and you could hear the pitch suddenly go higher, as the speed increased. When the pilot holes for the screws were drilled, it was accompanied by a screeching, grinding noise. A naive listener outside the OR door might think there was an auto body repair shop inside.

The anesthetic was straightforward. My chief concern was for Lidia to awaken without much pain. I wanted her to exit the OR with sufficient comfort to get her through the first few hours once surgery was completed, the hours when pain would be the most intense. My task was especially important, because the floor nurses, for reasons I never understood, were not permitted to give any narcotic once a patient had left the PACU.

When a patient was receiving what you considered a sufficient amount of anesthetic agent, a sharp rise in heart rate or blood pressure with intense surgical stimulation signaled the need for a narcotic. I gave several doses of fentanyl during the periods of bone work, the most painful parts of the operation, and by the time the wounds were being closed, Lidia's hemodynamics were steady. I had what we termed "railroad tracks" on my anesthetic record, steady horizontal lines recording blood pressure and heart rate that were little changing over the past half hour. I was satisfied I had just the right amount of narcotic on board for Lidia to awaken in comfort.

When the skin closure was complete, we still had another ten- or fifteen-minutes operative time, because Lidia needed to have casts applied to both lower legs. I pulled out her ETT and placed a facemask over her nose and mouth. I turned off my anesthetic gas, trying to time her awakening to coincide with the moment the surgeon stepped back and announced the plaster was dry and he was finished.

As I waited for the surgeon to complete his work, Mick, working on the table next to me, was ready to induce his next patient. His child was only five or six years old, and we always tried to help each other when we took care of kids that young. Fortunately, a fourth-year medical student had accompanied our mission team that week, so before I moved to the other operating table to assist with induction, I called him to my side.

"Here," I said. "Just hold this mask on her face as she wakes up. You can see that she's breathing by watching the anesthesia bag expand and collapse. Don't worry. I'll be just a few feet away, helping get this other patient to sleep." The student slid into my place and grabbed the mask. I looked back and assured myself Lidia was breathing fine.

As the second child was being induced, I heard whimpering from my own patient, as Lidia came out from under the anesthetic. I thought, damn it, I haven't given her near enough narcotic to wake up on. I looked to the medical student. "Ask her if she's hurting."

The student leaned over and did as instructed. She slowly shook her head back and forth, indicating "no." She began to cry.

I moved back to my table and took over the facemask. Now she was weeping forcefully. Tears were streaming to the sides of her cheeks. I bent over her, close to her head, and asked, "Are you hurting?" I removed the facemask so she could answer.

She again shook her head to the sides, this time vigorously, still sobbing. "Why are you crying?" I asked gently.

She continued to weep, seemingly unable to answer me.

I tried again, tenderly. "Lidia, can you tell me why you are crying?"

Between heaving breaths, she choked, "I'm normal! I'm normal!"

I looked up at the surgeon who was still molding the casts and swallowed hard. He cocked his head and shook it slowly. Neither of us spoke. I blinked rapidly to clear my eyes. A sudden lump in my throat felt as big as an apricot. An enormous sadness sprang up from within. I was astonished at the depths of my feelings. But looking back, how could it be otherwise? Lidia's response was heartbreaking and wondrous, painful, yet sublime. What would be normal for her? At best, with her feet fused and immobile, she would be able to stand upright and walk with a staggering gait. Her hands would remain like flippers. But that was enough for her. After a few moments, the surgeon and I spoke a few words to each other about something that meant nothing, which is what physicians do when the subject at hand is too poignant to acknowledge.

Like the little Gypsy boy who died, Lidia's memory has never strayed far from my path. I've thought often of what she said. It was humbling to witness it. I'm not sure which of us benefitted more from our brief interaction. Over the years, thinking of her has helped shape my own expectations. Maybe it's made me a little more normal, as well.

Chapter 10

UNFATHOMABLE

AFTER MY ROMANIA MISSION trip, I viewed my practice life differently. The things that previously annoyed me were now far less troubling. Even taking in-hospital overnight call, which I had always hated, I found easier. Many nights, no matter how late it was that I settled into bed in the Obstetrics Anesthesia Service call room, I consciously thought, well, you could be in Romania. I viewed my out-of-hospital life differently as well. I became more grateful for my blessings, for all the things I had been given or that had come to me easily—born American, brought up in a stable family, and all the rest.

Like most healthy people, I pretty much took my able physical condition for granted. Aside from a scare early in my career with a serious infection, I had had no major illnesses, and I expected to stay healthy for a long time. When I took care of patients who faced death, the idea of my own passing rarely entered my mind. When it did, it was as some kind of nebulous destination, so far away in the distance I couldn't really imagine ever going there. Like most people going through life who took their physical well being for granted, I needed to be reminded how quickly that could be taken away.

One Saturday on a beautiful spring day, I was on call for a 12-hour shift on obstetrics at our Women's hospital. I would cover any cases in the Women's OR as well, but there were none booked that day. My required work was done by noon—a couple of elective Caesarian-Sections and notes written on the patients who had been operated on the day before—and we had only three or four epidurals going for patients in labor. I had two very experienced CRNAs working on call with me, so I would not be needed for anything unless something really serious came up.

My pager went off. "Hey David. Saggio. Call me," followed by the hospital extension he was at. Mick Saggio, my partner from mission trips, was doing a 12-hour call shift at our main hospital, attached to Women's by a long corridor. The short, blunt message was typical of Mick.

I dialed the phone and he immediately picked up. "Mick, David here. What's going on?"

"I've got a lot. If you're not busy, come over to OR 10."

"No problem. I'm all caught up here."

He came back quickly. "Don't waste any time getting here."

That sounded serious. I quickly walked the couple hundred yards that connected the hospitals and went right to the surgical suite. Outside the OR 10 door, parked in the middle of the hallway, was an ICU bed. A portable monitor was tipped on its side, perched on sheets that were pulled halfway off the mattress. Whoever the patient was, I thought, they must have been moving fast.

As I opened the rear door to the room, the first thing that hit me was the smell—strong, foul. It was intense enough that I could almost taste it. Nothing good ever gave off that kind of aroma. In fact, the smell always signaled that something, some part of a patient, had died.

As I entered, I saw Dr. Bill Peacock bent over an abdominal incision that stretched all the way from the bottom of the sternum, or breastbone, to the pubis. "Shit." He spat the word out. "Shit. Shit." As he repeated it, he withdrew his arm from the open cavity, holding a surgical clamp. Dangling from the end was a grey, bloody strip of flesh. It looked as bad as it smelled. Whatever it was, it was indeed dead. "Shit," he repeated once more. He dropped the tissue onto a pile of similar strips that lay on a lap pad ("lap" being short for laparotomy, or abdominal)—cotton cloths that are used in belly operations to sop up blood or anything else that needs to be removed from the surgical site.

Bill looked up. "Shit, man. This is peritoneum. It's all like this. Shit." What he meant was, the dead tissue he was removing was from the outer lining of the abdominal cavity, a thin, normally clear glistening membrane. I had seen a lot of dead tissue come out of abdominal cavities over the years, but never the lining itself. Whatever had happened was devastating.

Across from Dr. Peacock stood Barry Britton, the surgical assistant. Barry was a big guy, always buoyant, always happy. Not now. He stared into the abdomen. His brow was creased.

"Hey Barry," I greeted him. I heard a grunt in return, but nothing else.

I looked to the head of the table. Randi Pough, the CRNA, bent over an arterial line transducer, drawing a blood sample into a syringe. Mick faced the monitor, looking up at the screen. The heart rate was fast, around 130. As soon as Randi flushed the arterial line, the pressure appeared on the screen. Low 80s systolic. Not very good. More serious was the shape—rounded hills as opposed to the steep little mountains they should have been. "More epi," Mick said, with weariness in his voice.

I announced my presence. "Hey, Mick. Whatcha got?"

Dr. Peacock heard my question and answered it for me. "Shit. And more shit. All kinda dead shit." Bill had a sarcastic, sardonic sense of humor, evidenced in almost everything he said. He wasn't trying to be funny.

Mick looked down from the monitor. "This lady is 42. On Wednesday she had liposuction up in the Atrium. Abdomen, flanks, thighs. Everything went well, or so they say. On Thursday, in the evening she went to an ER with abdominal pain. She was sent home, nothing to worry about. Friday, she got worse. Finally came in this morning, septic as hell. Looks like one of the trocars went in and punctured some bowel." The trocar was the long metal tube that was jammed into areas through which the unwanted fat was suctioned out. During the operation, it had somehow been misguided and pushed into the abdominal cavity, unnoticed, and torn a hole in her intestines. "Now we're here. Having a hard time holding her pressure, even with epi. And we've been fighting sky-high potassium. What's worse, is she's got two kids at home."

When you set about solving the equation of caring for a patient, there were a bunch of variables to plug in—the age, the sex, the medicines they were taking, the acuity of the problem, the chronic medical diseases the patient brought with them, and so forth—but personal details about their life weren't included. After all, whatever nonmedical things might be going on in a patient's life didn't really influence what you would be doing for them. So, only rarely would a report ever include some personal history of a patient. But this was rare in its tragedy.

The brief summary hit me hard. I could easily fill in the blanks, maybe getting a few details wrong, but regardless, for sure I'd get the ending right. A routine liposuction, totally elective. For the plastic surgeon, cosmetic cases didn't come any easier than sucking out the fat where a patient didn't want it. Sure, there was a little "art" involved in getting the contour of the skin nicely smooth where you worked, but not much. These cases were so easy you could do them with your eyes closed. Whatever the reason the lady chose for the procedure—dissatisfaction with her appearance, a present for her husband, her best friend had been so pleased with her results—didn't really matter. Everyone knew we did these all the time, in and out in a few hours, and in a healthy patient the only real concern was she might not be totally satisfied with the outcome. If she was some kind of a perfectionist, that could always be touched up later, if need be. The significant complications people think about when sick older patients are operated on like stroke, heart attack, or death—they didn't ever happen in patients like this. Until they did. And when they did, it was unfathomable. Even the ER physician had not suspected anything serious when she saw the patient and sent her back home on Thursday. Now, it might be too late.

Some things hit you so hard you think it will knock you over. Things that are so out of the accepted order, so wrong, that it hurts to even hear of them—murder, suicide, the death of a child, and here, a totally healthy woman with those two kids at home, who only wanted to be prettier, then life could go on just like before. Now, fighting for her life. Unfathomable. And unacceptable, other than we all had no choice but to accept what was happening and fight like hell for her.

Don't ever think your doctors, your nurses, your aides, and anyone else involved in patient care doesn't feel the same emotions in these horrible situations that you do. We are all part of the same devastating humanity.

"How can I help?" I asked.

For the next twenty minutes I pitched in, but I really didn't add to the woman's care. It was pretty easy to figure out what to do. What wasn't so easy was to control what was happening. As Dr. Peacock pulled out the dead tissue that lined her abdominal cavity, the potassium level in her blood rose to a dangerous level. Potassium (or simply K^+, and often referred to as "Kay") is an ion that influences the way the electrical signal travels through the heart. Too little, and the heart will fibrillate, contracting like a mass of worms without squeezing any blood out of it. Too much, and the heart will stop. We gave her the usual treatments for high K^+- bicarbonate, a combination of glucose and insulin, some calcium chloride—but we couldn't control its inexorable march upwards. Finally, as it rose up above 7, her heart rate slowed, and then the conduction impulse totally ceased flowing through the muscle. And with that, her heart stopped beating. The monitor showed the flat ECG trace crawling across it that you have likely seen on television dramas. The arterial trace was flat as well.

"There she goes," one of us said.

Dr. Peacock repeated, "Shit."

He stepped back from the operating table. Barry leaned over, placed his hands on the chest, one over the other, and began pumping downward at a rate of around a hundred times a minute, grunting, "One, two, three." We gave an ampule of epinephrine and then an ampule of sodium bicarbonate. She remained stopped. We added a gram of calcium chloride. Finally, electrical activity resumed, and we could see small pulsations from the arterial line on the monitor.

"Stop pumping," Mick commanded.

Then he added, "Let's go up on her epi." Randi increased the infusion rate of the drug that was keeping the blood pressure up.

After another ten or fifteen minutes, she arrested again.

"Shit."

We got her back, pretty quickly that time.

But within fifteen minutes, she arrested a third time.

"Shit."

We got her back, but it took longer.

Mick breathed a weary sigh and looked pensive, lost in thought. Finally, he spoke. "Bill, we can't keep her K$^+$ down. No matter what we do, it keeps going up. We've even given her some nebulized albuterol. I can't think of anything else to do but get her to the ICU and put her on dialysis. Even with that, I'm not sure we'll win this race."

Dr. Peacock looked up, his clamp holding yet another strip of dead tissue, blood and pus dripping from it. "I'll never get all of this shit out of here. Yeah, I think maybe we close her up and get her upstairs."

With that, her surgery was done. Not completed, but stopped.

Normally, an abdominal incision was closed carefully, in several layers, ending up with the skin being the last. Dr. Peacock abandoned that approach in favor of speed, as he bunched the sides of the wound together with large, interrupted stitches that went through all the layers at once. The closure was far from ideal, but he would take her back to surgery in a day or two if we could keep her alive upstairs, if we could somehow keep that K$^+$ down.

One of us placed a dialysis catheter underneath her collarbone as Dr. Peacock finished sewing her up. As it was being sutured in place, she arrested again.

"Shit."

We got her back again. A potassium sample we drew when the dialysis catheter went in showed the level was 7.4. That was no worse than the one prior. Maybe there was hope.

One of us said, "I wonder if we should slip a pacemaker wire in through the neck. It would be nice to just be able to pace her out of her arrest."

Someone replied, "Let's not take the time. We can always pace her externally if we need to. Right now, she needs dialysis if she has any chance of getting through this."

We rushed the ICU bed into the room. Within ten minutes we got her upstairs to the Unit where a dialysis machine was waiting. The tech stood like a sentry at its side, solemn.

I didn't have any duties awaiting me, and I had no special place to go, but I needed to get away. Thankfully, I didn't see any family as I left the ICU and hustled down to the doctor's lounge.

Around twenty minutes later, Mick shuffled in. He looked beaten, like someone had knocked him to the floor and he'd just managed to pick himself up. We looked at each other, but neither spoke. I figured he was thinking the same thing I was—we are all one small step away from the proof of our own mortality. We'd better appreciate every day as a gift, and tonight we should go home and tell our families we loved them. Mick ate a sandwich while I ate some Cheetos. For some reason, when I was on call and especially anxious, or when something terrible was anticipated, I ate Cheetos. I finished the bag and opened another.

Around an hour later, I went to the ICU to place a central line (those were IVs placed deep in the jugular vein or other internal veins in which powerful cardiac drug infusions could be safely given) in a patient. Mick had several on his list of requested lines, and I had time to help him out. Our ICU was divided into four "pods," each containing eight beds. I was working in the B pod, separated by a short open hallway to A pod where our liposuction patient had been delivered. As I finished my work, I tentatively asked the nurse assisting me, "Do you know how the lady in A is doing that we brought up earlier?"

She replied, "Not very well. They can't get that potassium down, even with dialysis. I know the family has been up to see her. They say it doesn't look good."

I thought about those two kids at home. How old were they? Had they been among the family members who came up? What's wrong with mom? Can she hear us? Mom? I tried to block it out. I couldn't.

I stepped to the desk to write a note in the chart. All at once, I heard a scream from A. And then, several people screaming. And then, a frightful moan. Deep, low, mournful. Almost rumbling. I thought, if a moan could emerge from your soul, that's what it would sound like. It was the kind of sound that could only result from something truly horrible.

A nurse came running into B pod from A. She was sobbing. She cried out, "It's over! It's over!"

I finished my note and left the ICU as quickly as possible, taking the long way around to avoid A.

It's been over fifteen years since that patient died, but from time to time, I think back about that woman and those two kids. It's not intentional, but something triggers it, like seeing a commercial on TV with a young mom serving her children at the breakfast table. I can still recall the nurse running into B, the sounds of those screams, the sound of that moan, just like my memory of the first time a bully pushed me down in the grade school playground. They recur in my mind, unwanted, unexpected, like a sudden storm on a sunny day.

Chapter 11

PERSPECTIVE

DESPITE MY RELIGIOUS FOUNDATION, losses like the young mother following routine liposuction still left me with a series of "what if's" that were deeply disquieting. It didn't matter that such deaths were rare, that the odds of them occurring were miniscule. For that young mother with the two kids, the incidence of mortality was one hundred per cent. What if the cannula had not been tilted too deeply on that one pass, might she still be alive, her biggest concern being how well those two kids were doing in school? What if the surgeon had noticed the cannula angling quite deep and obtained an abdominal x-ray in the PACU, just to be on the safe side? Might he have found the bowel perforation and brought her back to surgery immediately? Would those two kids still have a mother? What if a different ER physician had been on duty when she was seen the evening after surgery? Might the correct diagnosis have been made and the young mother saved? In the end, I simply came to accept tragedies like what had befallen that patient as sad, catastrophic, yet inevitable aspects of life. You witnessed them, you felt them, and then you moved on as best you could.

One thing you experienced, as soon as you received your medical degree, was the power of the doctor-patient relationship. It began with patients trusting you as an intern to take care of them, innocent of your ineptness. Their belief in your abilities only grew stronger as you gained experience and actually became proficient at what you were doing. Their trust often allowed physicians to make decisions about a patient's health care almost at will, even though they might both pretend that each side had an equal say. If you backed away and viewed it from a distance, though, one of the most remarkable aspects of the relationship doctors had with those they cared for was how disproportionately the power was distributed in the connection. On the physician side was pretty much all the dominance—the knowledge, the skills, the judgment, the experience, the confidence, the execution. We even spoke our own secret language, with hold over Latin terms such as "decubitus" and "dolor" and "per os." All that was needed was to tell the patient what you were going to do and then go do it. The only real control patients had was to leave your care and go get another doctor. But they hardly ever knew when that might be wise. In the end, patients were pretty much at the mercy of their doctors.

Almost all the doctors I practiced with during my time in medicine used the power they had with patients wisely. For surgeons, most simply recommended what they would wish for their own family. That made giving advice pretty easy. In fact, it was fairly common for me or someone I was with to say to a patient something like, "Well, if you were my brother . . . "

Even after many years in private practice, I didn't really know what it felt like to be a patient or a family going through a medical crisis. In order to appreciate that helpless perspective, I would have to share their experience, and no one in my immediate family nor I had ever had major surgery. That would change.

One day I caught Dr. Frank Berman between cases, striding out of the doctor's lounge where he had dictated his first case. Frank was a big guy, imposing, with big hands, a big voice, and a big heart. He was a typical orthopedic surgeon: just give me a bone to saw on and I'll be happy, a "what you see is what you get" kind of doctor. He always had a smile and always had a sparkle in his eye. Always something nice to say.

Earlier that week I had received a book in the mail from Frank along with a note of thanks, saying he really appreciated what I had done. I had no idea what he was referring to. It was unusual to receive a present from a surgeon, so I said good morning and asked, "Frank, thank you for the book you sent me. But what's that all about?"

He stopped, looked at me intently, seriously, then said, "Remember that guy you helped me with last week? The one who almost didn't make it off the table? The one with DIC? That's the third case I've had like that. The first two died."

My mind traced back. About ten days earlier I'd finished a long cardiac case at around 2 pm. I was then assigned three orthopedic rooms and told to relieve Dr. Arnold Pugh, the anesthesiologist supervising them, and send him home.

I made my way to the first two ORs, signed the records, and familiarized myself with the anesthetics. Both were routine. When I entered OR 6, it was far different. I immediately heard a suction device slurping and swishing up blood from the surgical field, making a distinctive sound as if someone were sucking in air through clenched teeth with his mouth half filled with water. In most operations, a surgeon would put a suction catheter into a wound from time to time to draw away blood that had slowly accumulated, but if you left it in the wound and the sound was constant, well, the bleeding was constant, too. I hurried to the head of the operating table and saw that the suction canister where the blood was collecting was about two thirds full. That was a lot of blood. The top third was all foam—an angry red milkshake—caused by blood continuously splashing into the container. Next to it was a second canister that had been swapped out from the collection system after it had completely filled. I thought, man, there's got to be five or six units in those two containers.

The IV pole that held the canister, as well as the one next to it, must have had 20 or 30 surgical sponges hanging from them, clipped one by one like laundry out to dry, little red flags soaked with blood. There were a few larger bloody lap pads hanging as well, suspended to visually assist in approximating blood loss, but also to keep accurate count of them, lest one be forgotten and left in the wound when the case was over and the patient was sewn up.

Dr. Berman, his head bobbing back and forth as he tried to get a better view, was bent over the lower back of a middle-aged male patient. He was calling for sponges as quickly as he was removing them. As they were taken out, I could see they were drenched. "Sponge. Another. Gimme another," he barked.

Along with suction, Frank was using a Bovie, an electrical device with a narrow tip that heated up tissues and blood vessels until they melted together, stopping bleeding like a solder gun would fuse a wire onto a circuit board. I could hear a snap and pop as it cooked tissue. A trail of smoke wafted up, filling the air with the smell of charred meat and burned fat.

I reached the head of the table and found Madeline Conrad, a CRNA with whom I had worked for over 20 years. She was exceptionally skilled and also a pretty cool customer, having done her share of high-risk surgeries with me over the years. Madeline was busy hanging a unit of blood, and I noticed another unit was already suspended and almost completely in via a second IV. She glanced up briefly, wide eyed. Her voice quivered as she said, "Dr. Alfery, we're in big trouble here. We've got uncontrolled bleeding. I've barely seen Dr. Pugh since this case started. I called out several times for him to come to the room, but he hasn't responded."

I fumed. There was no excuse for Pugh not being there. When you were called to a room, you came to the room. Period. He had probably been told I would be relieving him, and like a horse smelling the hay and heading for the barn, he likely had one foot out the door. I couldn't worry about him, though. Madeline needed help, and by the looks of things, a lot of it.

As she pressurized a bag around the unit of blood so it would run in faster, Madeline gave me a quick update: multilevel back decompression with instrumentation, now around two and a half hours into it. The initial bleeding had been minor but steady. Now, it was massive. Over the past 30 minutes at least five units of blood lost, likely more, and she was getting more and more behind with her transfusions. Dr. Berman was doing his best to stop it, but he was having little success. "Sponge, goddamn it," he repeated. Then, "Move the suction here. No, no, damn it. Here!" There was no doubt—the patient was bleeding to death.

I looked up at the gas vaporizer to see how much anesthetic the patient was receiving. It was a pretty low concentration, considerably less than you'd expect to give for a patient undergoing back surgery. Madeline has cut back, I thought, trying to keep the blood pressure up.

Anesthetists knew that you needed to achieve three things in getting your patient through surgery. First, you had to keep the patient from moving. You could do that with a muscle relaxant, but it's simply safer to give enough agent that a patient doesn't move when stimulated. (On many occasions, when someone outside medicine asked what I did in the OR, I said, "I just hold them still for the surgeon to operate on.") Second, you needed the patient unconscious, to not remember anything that was going on. Third, you needed to have the hemodynamics—the patient's blood pressure and heart rate—controlled. Reducing the amount of anesthetic you gave, "lightening" the anesthetic, resulted in an increase in both heart rate and pressure. These signs vary as if the patient were crying out to alert you that he was not getting enough anesthetic agent. By cutting back on the amount of gas she was giving, Madeline was getting the patient to help (even though he was asleep) keep the blood pressure up. Of course, a danger that came with lowering the gas concentration was that one might get a patient light enough that he or she would remember being operated on, a condition we described with the sanitized name "awareness." That experience is unspeakably horrible—imagine feeling your body being cut on, being unable to move, and a breathing tube between your vocal cords preventing your scream being heard. We used a brain monitor to alert us of that danger, but it wasn't 100 per cent reliable.

The unit of blood Madeline had hung just as I arrived was the last she had immediately available. She had called for more, but it hadn't yet arrived. The blood pressure was hanging precipitously, with the systolic in the 80s, like someone grasping on to a ledge by his or her fingertips. Madeline had been able to keep the pressure from falling even further by giving repeated doses of neosynephrine, a drug that constricted blood vessels and provided at least temporary support, but the doses had become higher and more frequently spaced together. The pulse oximeter beeped out a rate of around 120 beats per minute, faster than normal as the heart beat reflexively increased, trying to keep tissues perfused and the blood pressure up.

I did a quick mental calculation of how much blood had been lost compared with how much Madeline had given back, trying to determine just how far behind we were, but that was hopeless. The textbooks told you to look at the suction canisters, the bloody sponges, and the operative field to estimate blood loss, but that was good only in, well, textbooks. Estimating how much a blood-soaked sponge held within it was notoriously inaccurate, and you couldn't account for the blood that had dripped off Dr. Berman's gown onto the floor and what was in the drapes surrounding the wound, or what was still pooled inside the wound cavity that you couldn't even see. Even the canisters were misleading, with foam making the fluid level within them indistinct. Once you got over, say, losing one half or more of the blood volume in the body, you really had no way of knowing what the total was. Our patient was well past that point. In situations like this, you simply hung replacement units as quickly as you could until you stopped needing to support the blood pressure with drugs.

When a patient is bleeding to death, the more IVs you have the better. I leaned down to the patient's right arm and snapped a rubber tourniquet around it. A vein came up on the back of his hand, and I rammed a 16-guage IV cannula in, giving us a third transfusion route. Before hooking up the intravenous line Madeline had assembled, I drew coagulation and blood count studies. I handed the blood tubes to the circulating nurse and said, "I need these run STAT. And we need those four units from the blood bank right now. They should be ready, but if not, I want them "emergency release." And have the lab run an INR, platelet count, a fibrinogen level, and a 'crit" (studies that would help identify deficiencies in blood clotting factors and give us a ballpark figure of the patient's blood volume status)." Emergency release units were those in which the major blood type had been shown to be the same as the patient's (either type O, A, B, or AB), but they didn't have time to be screened for minor antibodies. You could get a mild transfusion reaction with them, but having the correct overall type prevented the major life-threatening ones. You transfused type-specific blood only in a crisis. I added, "Also, let's get four FFP, a six-pack of plate-lets, and ten units of cryo. I'd like them twenty minutes ago, please, so STAT, STAT. Oh, and tell the blood bank to stay six units ahead."

"Six ahead?" she questioned. To ask for that many units of blood to be set up, in addition to the four that were coming, was almost unheard of. Also, I knew the blood bank would complain about releasing all those clot-ting products—fresh frozen plasma (FFP), platelets, and cryoprecipitate (a blood product with a high concentration of a vital clotting factor called fibrinogen—we called it "cryo")—without first having abnormal lab values to justify it. But we simply couldn't afford to wait for the results to come back and confirm what we already knew—the patient needed all of them. The studies would prove useful in guiding us as to how much of the factors would be needed, and we would get a head start without them.

Frank looked up and said, "Dave, I've got a lot of bleeding here. I can't control it. I can't find anything obvious. It seems to be coming from every-where. And he's not making any clots at all." This was the first time I'd ever heard Dr. Berman sound frightened. Like most orthopedic surgeons, he was always steady, always calm, always in control. And like most surgeons with oversized personalities, he was always commanding in the room when operating.

Fear can spread quickly, moving like a prairie fire with the wind blow-ing hard. Part of my job as an anesthesiologist is to keep that fire from engulfing the entire operating team, so that the operator can focus entirely on his job at hand.

I nodded and spoke calmly, hiding the terror I felt inside. "We've given what blood we have, and we have more on the way. We're behind right now, so anything you can do to temporize would help."

There was no point in admitting just how far behind we were.

I added, "Can you throw some lap pads in there and just hold pressure until we get more blood in the room?"

Sometimes a surgeon trying to control bleeding could be half paralyzed, suctioning more and more blood out of the wound without really stopping any of it. I needed Frank to cease his efforts and just hold the cloth pads firmly against the tissues to physically prevent more hemorrhage until we caught up with our transfusions.

Frank grunted his assent.

My ability to walk into the room and seamlessly insert myself into the case was partly due to Madeline's understanding of what was going on, but it was also a result of the relationship I had with Dr. Berman. During the many years we had worked together, we had both achieved a vital component of the glue that held surgeons and anesthesiologists together—trust. Surgeons had enough on their hands when they had to fight for the life of a patient, as Frank was doing, without having to worry about what was going on at the head of the table.

At its best, the relationship between a surgeon and an anesthesiologist is like a good marriage. If you worked with a surgeon consistently, you might even spend more time with each other than with your spouse. You might hear your counterpart begin a sentence and be able to finish it for them. As in a marriage, you are considerate of the other's wishes, you anticipate the other's needs, you respect the other's abilities, you know the other's weaknesses, you strive for a common goal. And as in most marriages, you likely fight from time to time, but you always make up, if only for the sake of the children (in this case, the patients).

I glanced at the blood pressure. The systolic was hovering in the 70s, way too low for safety. I dialed back the gas concentration some more.

I was pretty certain the patient had a condition called DIC, or disseminated intravascular coagulopathy. DIC was a grave disorder, life threatening. In DIC, the clotting factors are quickly consumed, leaving the patient unable to form new clots to stop their bleeding. The treatment for DIC is to resupply the body with adequate clotting factors—FFP, platelets, cryoprecipitate—by transfusion, to get enough in so that clots would again form. That would allow Frank to identify any discrete vessels that were still bleeding and stop them. If we couldn't do all that, this patient would die in the OR, just like Dr. Berman's other two patients with DIC had.

Dr. Pugh finally poked his head through the door. He didn't even step into the room, but simply leaned in and asked, "Am I good to go?" I was angry. I wanted to grill him over where he'd been, but I waved him off, not wanting to take the time.

I checked the blood pressure again—unchanged—and I nervously dialed the anesthetic gas concentration even lower. I was trying to keep the patient just barely asleep, just barely deep enough that he wouldn't remember being cut on, but still light enough that he could provide all the help he could in keeping his pressure up.

Soon, Madeline and I were well into giving the patient the additional four units of red cells and the first round of clotting factors I'd asked for. As we worked, Frank continued to ask—almost pleading—for help. "Suction! Losing suction!" And then, "Another lap pad, to the left!" Then, "No suction! The suction's not working! Get my damn suction working!" The circulating nurse sprinted across the room and found the suction canister filled to the top with blood, so she quickly replaced it with a fresh, empty one. As the suction resumed, it seemed louder to me than it should have, almost like the rapids of a river churning through a canyon. Because continuous suctioning of blood indicates uncontrolled bleeding, I think there is a tendency to somehow magnify its sound in your head, as if your mind is yelling at you, "Listen to that! Listen how loud that damn suction is! Transfuse faster!"

Over the next hour, Madeline and I gave almost 60 units of blood and blood products while Frank struggled to stop the bleeding. When you hear a total like that in the news, it doesn't mean 60 units of red blood cells, but rather the total of the units of blood, FFP, platelets, and cryoprecipitate that are transfused. Still, it constituted way more than two entire blood volumes of the patient. During that frantic time, there was none of the usual bantering that goes on in the OR. Just the constant sound of suction.

At one point, I dialed the gas back so far that the numerical read-out on the brain monitor showed the patient to be right at the edge of awakening. I gave a dose of Versed, hoping it would provide a period of amnesia until we could dial it back up. If the patient did experience a period of awareness—and provided he lived through this operation—I would simply tell him what we had been forced to do to keep him alive.

Madeline and I pumped blood and blood products into the patient as fast as we could, using all three IVs. Then we pumped some more. As we crept closer to replacing the patient's deficits, I occasionally reported to Frank, "We're keeping up pretty well, now." Frank responded, "I think I see some clot here!" I suspect we were trying to reassure ourselves as much as each other that we were gaining ground.

As you fight to gain control in a case like this, you do your best to stay focused on all the medical issues at hand: how far behind are you, what about the urine output, is he deep enough with his anesthetic, when should the next dose of antibiotic be given since he is bleeding out what's in his bloodstream, do I need some bicarbonate for his acidosis, and much more. But even as you try to stay totally dialed in, there is an occasional voice that intrudes, asking: I wonder if this guy is going to die? Will we lose the battle? Will his death be a direct failure on my part, that I simply didn't do enough, right enough, fast enough? Even though your intellect assures you that you would have done all you could, your emotional side whispers its protest. And like a stone tossed into a pond that causes ripples in all directions, you're subtly aware of all the lives the death of the patient would affect: the wife, the parents, the kids, the friends.

What allows you to function without going all to pieces is your ability to view the situation as managing a case rather than treating an individual. You take the distanced perspective of a person of science dealing with a clinical problem with cold intellect, dehumanizing it as much as possible.

You may think it callous that physicians can view their patients in extremis with little emotion, but were it otherwise, sick patients would never get proper care. And because physicians can never view their own families without looking through a lens of feeling, they should never care for their own loved ones.

During our struggle to replace the blood the patient was losing, I lost track of time. I couldn't tell if we had been working for 30 minutes or 130. I just knew we couldn't let up for a second.

But Frank gradually got control of the bleeding—"Getting there!" he cried out. "I think it's slowing down!"—and the mood in the room lightened. At last, solid clots began to form, and the bleeding was, indeed, slowed. Frank sang out like a child at his birthday party, "I like what I'm seeing here! This is good! This is so good!"

I cautiously increased the anesthetic.

After another fifteen minutes, bleeding had all but ceased, and the patient was stable. We had caught up with our transfusions, and the actual operation could resume. Frank looked at me. I gave him a 'thumbs up' sign. "Glad the fun part's over," I said.

Over the next hour, Frank completed his instrumentation and started to close the wound. "A little closing music, if you please," he asked the circulating nurse. That meant the stressful part was done and everyone could relax to some celebratory, upbeat tunes, perhaps classic Bob Seger or maybe Jimmy Buffet.

The area around the operating table was a mess, as if an animal had been slaughtered—smears of blood on the floor, scores of red-caked sponges hanging on IV poles, lap pads stacked and stuck together, canisters filled with blood in a neat row to the side, and bloody shoe prints leading out the door. The unmistakable metallic, ferric smell of blood, caused by the iron in the hemoglobin that carries oxygen to our bodies, hung in the air. As the skin stitches were being placed, I arranged for the patient to be transferred directly to the ICU with the breathing tube still in place. Given all that he had been through, we would keep him asleep overnight and take the tube out in the morning.

Madeline prepared to move the patient to a bed for transport while I stripped off my gloves. We had been at it continuously for almost three hours. When I turned to leave, Madeline leaned over and said, "Dr. Alfery, thank you for not leaving me." It was a nice thing to say, though she knew I never would. I felt the same gratitude for her dedication, and I expressed that to her. That case was a perfect example of why I spent my entire practice life working with superb CRNAs: when we faced a crisis, we had two heads and four hands at work at the head of the operating table.

I left the room and stopped in the hallway. I was spent. I slumped down and squatted, with my back resting against the wall, my arms crossed and perched on my knees. I lowered my head and rested it on my forearms. I closed my eyes and reflected for a moment. One word kept coming into my mind. Alive!

I didn't know why Dr. Berman's other two patients with DIC had died. Perhaps their bleeding had been more torrential? Maybe they'd had someone like Dr. Pugh at the head of the table or lacked an experienced CRNA like Madeline? Whatever the reason, I was just grateful our patient made it through. Not only had the patient lived, but he also had no memory of even being in the OR.

"Well, Frank," I said, "you certainly didn't need to send me anything for that case. I mean, we just do what we do, you know? It was pretty wild in there for a while."

Frank looked at me thoughtfully. "I know," he replied. "But the other two I've had like that died on the table. Oh, I sent Madeline something, as well."

Over the next two years, I managed a couple other patients in the OR with DIC, but they weren't associated with back surgery. Neither had as massive a bleed as Dr. Berman's patient, and thankfully, each survived. But I never lost my respect for how hazardous DIC cases could be.

In the 19th century, the term "heroic medicine" came into use, referring to dramatic, often experimental attempts to reverse the course of a disease. It always struck me as odd—applying the term "heroic" to the medical team, as if they were the ones taking the risk, like fire fighters running into a burning building. But no matter how harrowing a physician's day, or how much anguish will persist after a close call (or worse), the doctor almost always gets to go home to his friends and family, and to carry on his life mostly as before.

Not so when the patient is a loved one. Having someone near and dear to you be caught in a life-threatening situation is the only way a doctor—even a caring one—can appreciate just what the families of desperately ill patients go through.

About two years after the case with Dr. Berman, my eighteen-year-old daughter Allison was scheduled for surgery at Vanderbilt Children's Hospital to correct her scoliosis, a curvature and bending forward of her spine that had progressed so much that further curvature would impair her breathing. The procedure was called Harrington rod instrumentation, and it would be a "double," one complete operation followed immediately by a second. In the first, a team of general surgeons would go into her abdomen and expose the lumbar spine in order for the orthopedic team to apply metal fixation to the bones. Following that, and while still anesthetized, Alli would be turned onto her stomach, and an operation similar to the one Dr. Berman did would be performed. In fact, the second operation was significantly larger than what Frank had done, with rods extending all the way from her upper to her lower back. The two procedures were expected to take ten hours total to complete. That amount of surgery all at once made me anxious, but that was how the Harrington rod operations were done at Vanderbilt, and I found it best to never ask skilled and experienced doctors to alter their routine. I had chosen the pediatric anesthesiologist, Dr. Jenny Adams, with care, as well as the orthopedic surgeon, and they both assured me that serious complications, even with combined surgeries, were rare.

On the day of the procedure, I took the day off from work and joined my wife at the hospital. Alli was scheduled to go into the OR around 7 am, so ideally, the surgery would be over around 5 pm. We kissed Alli as the stretcher was rolled towards the OR, and then Joyce and I settled into the waiting room, carving out a little corner where we would spend the day, newspaper and books in hand. It felt strange to be there as a family member. When I went into medicine, I had naively thought that being a doctor would give me an inside track that could shield me from the frailties and uncertainties everyone seemed to experience when faced with a serious illness or operation. I found reality to be the opposite. While my education allowed me to navigate the waters of medicine with greater ease, I was cursed with knowing how many places the ship could run aground. The thought of all the problems the surgical teams might encounter intruded in my mind as my wife and I sat together, but I kept them to myself. When Joyce expressed her fears over the complexity and length of the two operations, I reminded her of all the similar cases I had done, and I emphasized that Alli was in the best of hands.

During the day, various friends stopped by to offer support, but I could hardly focus on their conversations. Every hour a nurse would come out to the waiting room and give us a progress report. I had always known, intellectually, that it was important to let a patient's family know how surgeries were advancing, but I had never *felt* it before. I couldn't help but think back to all the surgeries I had been involved in where a report was seldom sent out, or even not at all.

Around 10 am the nurse appeared. She looked happy. "Things are moving along really well," she reported. "The anterior fixation is already done, and the general surgeons are closing the abdomen." One down, I thought, one to go.

By midafternoon the posterior fixation was completed, and the nurse appeared to announce that they were beginning to close up her back. I breathed a sigh of relief. Home free.

Except we weren't. Just after 4 p.m. the nurse came out again, this time looking grim. Joyce looked up, anxiously; I stood up.

"There's been a problem with bleeding," the nurse said, curtly. "They've called for the general surgeon to go back into the abdomen to correct it. We'll keep you informed." I felt my knees buckle, but I straightened quickly. The nurse turned abruptly and hurried away, leaving us no time to even ask a question.

"What does that mean?" Joyce demanded. "Is this serious?"

"Oh, these things happen," I casually lied, trying to sound reassuring. "I suspect there's a little bleeder in there they have to coagulate or tie off, and then they'll be done." Maybe there *was* a little bleeder in there, I tried to tell myself. But maybe she'd developed full-blown DIC? Then again, how likely was that? In close to twenty years of practice, I could count on one hand the number of times I'd treated DIC in spine operations. Maybe two, three at the most. But still, my heart raced. I thought back to Frank's comment: "The first two died." In my mind, I stacked my experience against his: none of my patients had ever died from DIC.

I said a silent prayer. Joyce and I spent the next hour with awkward small talk.

Sixty minutes passed without an update. That was the first time they missed their unspoken schedule. Then an hour and a half. This meant that the nurse could not afford to leave the OR for even a couple of minutes. I felt nauseous. This was no simple bleeder to tie off. My heart pounded as if it would beat clear out of my chest; my mouth felt parched. I swallowed, but there was nothing to go down. I visualized the operating room and could picture what had happened. First, an unexpected fall in blood pressure while Alli's back was being closed. The pressure stayed down, despite lightening the anesthesia and increasing her IV fluids. Then a further fall, this one alarming, that required correction by a large dose of a vasopressor. Then a hand slipped under the drapes to feel the abdomen, just to be sure. Then, suddenly, upon encountering the belly stretched tense with shed blood, a scramble to finish the back closure, skipping some deep sutures and zipping her up with skin staples, calling the general surgeons STAT, flipping my daughter onto her back, and splashing betadine antiseptic onto her abdomen. Then frantically slashing her belly open and finding the inside filled with blood. Dialing the anesthetic concentration lower, and then, dialing it lower still, then seeing the brain monitor right at the edge of waking up. The emergency call for blood units and clotting factors, even before coags had been sent, with each being transfused as fast as possible, sponges being hung out to dry like little red flags, a canister full of suctioned blood being replaced with a new empty one, and all the rest.

Running through the scene in my mind, I felt like I might pass out. Part of me wanted to rush to the doctor's dressing room, change into scrubs, burst into the OR, and announce I was there to lend a hand. I realized how absurd that was, but I was desperate. I thought, so *this* is how families feel when things turn terrible. Helpless. I was totally at the mercy of those taking care of Alli and whatever role fate might play in the process.

I wondered if I should share my concerns with Joyce, but in the end, I decided not to burden her. Finally, at around 6:30 pm the nurse reappeared. She looked relieved. She told us how Alli had lost quite a lot of blood, that she had "developed a condition known as DIC," but the bleeding was finally under control. She thought within an hour Alli would be in the ICU. But with all Alli had been through, they would leave the breathing tube in overnight. The description was all too painfully familiar to me. I turned to Joyce with tears in my eyes. We reached out and held each other tight.

An hour and a half later, the nurse brought us in to see her. She looked like countless other patients I had cared for over the years in the ICU—tubes and wires coming out in seemingly all directions, and deeply asleep while the ventilator gave a "whoosh" and the pulse oximeter sounded its tone. But I also saw in her, and maybe fully for the first time, a real, whole person lying in an ICU bed. Like so much of life, until you've been there, you never really know.

A few days after surgery, once she was out of the ICU, I reviewed with Alli's anesthesiologist the events in the OR—the unexpected bleeding, the frantic transfusion of clotting factors, her struggle to keep up, and the scare that Alli had given the entire OR team. I thanked her for her diligence and expertise. And I especially thanked her for staying until Alli was safely transported into the PACU, long after when the on-call anesthesiologist could have relieved her. I briefly wondered if she felt the same kind of fear in the OR that I did in a life-threatening circumstance. How could she not? It's just part of being human. And when the worst was over and it was clear that Alli would live through the bleeding, did the anesthesiologist respond in a manner similar to me? Did she pause, exhausted and spent, thinking of just one word? Alive!

Chapter 12

DESPERATION

AFTER MY DAUGHTER ALMOST bled to death in the OR, I could *really* understand what other families went through when a loved one's life was on the line. It made me far more aware of the need for updates being sent out to the family as surgery progressed. I could also better empathize with a parent as I carried their young son or daughter off to the OR. I looked back to my medical missions, and I remembered the times when a mother gave me—a total stranger, a foreigner to boot—her child to care for.

Most of the medical missions that Dr. Mick Saggio and I went on together were with an organization called Operation Smile. That work was particularly rewarding because they operated primarily on cleft lips and palates in children. The facial deformities were some of the most severe imaginable, including some clefts that extended all the way up into the nose, turning the face into a grotesque, Halloween monster mask. Surgery for those children was life changing. As Mick once told me, "David, it's an hour and a half of our life. It's the rest of their life."

In order for a child to be operated on, he or she first had to get through a screening process, a week prior to the week when the surgeries were to be performed. Three or four hundred children might show up for screening, having traveled from the farthest reaches of their country. Kids who had only minor deformities or had significant medical problems to go along with their facial abnormalities were generally turned down. For those that were fortunate enough to be chosen, the families would stay on over the weekend and then get their operation one day the following week. From the time of travel to the hospital until their postoperative recovery, they might spend almost two weeks near the hospital. During that period, many families simply slept outside on the ground, or once their child was operated on, crowded into a small hospital room along with other patients and other family members.

For our trip to Managua, Nicaragua, we worked in a run-down hospital that probably dated back to the forties, the fifties at the latest, on a run-down street, in a run-down part of the city. But it had enough of what we needed to spend five long days running five operating rooms from morning until evening, repairing the lucky ones.

As an anesthesiologist whose practice consisted almost entirely of adults, I was anxious about caring for the youngest patients. Their veins were so tiny and their airways so small, I felt clumsy. There was little room for error when you anesthetized them, and when things went bad, they went bad in a hurry. Young children don't have the reserve that older patients have. In addition, in the OR we didn't have all the modern equipment we were used to back home. Fortunately, most of the kids were at least a couple of years old, but invariably, we would have a few that were infants. The very youngest were always the first case of the day on Monday, our first day of surgeries, so my anxiety level peaked as the mission week began. At least the worst would be over right away.

Looking back, it never really dawned on me that, regardless of how frightened I was to be taking care of a baby in a third world country, it had to be far more difficult for the parents. They were desperate. Almost all who brought their children in for evaluation were poor and spoke no English. Their kids had facial deformities that, without repair, would prevent them from ever having a chance at a normal life. They would be ridiculed, shunned. There would be no public schooling or normal socialization. No life at all. For those chosen, there was none of the detailed anesthesia informed consent that was done back home. In fact, there was no real discussion about anesthesia at all. Had they known that, though rare, there was a chance of death when you operated on children in these circumstances, I'm certain they would have all chosen to proceed, anyway. I suspect some would have gone forward even if a death were not rare. Our mission was their only hope.

Imagine surrendering your child to medical practitioners who were in your country for a single week, who had appeared, seemingly out of nowhere. All you really knew was that your anguished prayers had been answered. You were told in your native tongue by a nurse to appear with your child in a large waiting room in the hospital the next day. When their name was called, you would entrust your child to a doctor you had met only a moment before, who would disappear down a hospital corridor. Likely, the doctor could not even acknowledge you with any words in your own language.

On the morning of the first day of surgery in Nicaragua, I paced. It was 8:10 am, and the cases were supposed to begin at 7:30 am. But as with most missions, the first day was already running behind, with last minute changes to the operating schedule and other logistics being worked out. My first patient would be less than a year old, and two years had passed since I had cared for an infant that young.

My circulating room nurse was named Julie, and she waited with me at the front desk of the operating suite. Like most of the people on the mission trip, Julie had come from a different part of the country than I and didn't know any of the other thirty-five members who had assembled for the week. We would be together all day, each day, and would be fast friends by the time Friday rolled around. On Saturday, we would depart, never to see each other again. The other surgical teams were milling around with us. We were lucky this year, because each crew had been assigned their own operating room, rather than having two surgeries done simultaneously, as I had with a prior mission.

We waited.

As we stood at the desk, I tried to mask my apprehension. It was bad enough to feel it—I didn't want to show it. I rocked back and forth on my feet and opened my hands widely, fingers stretched apart, then clenched them in fists, as if that might calm me. No luck. "Damn it," I murmured, "can't we just get started and get the first little one done?"

Then, all at once, five young mothers holding infants in their arms arrived, led by a hospital nurse. They walked towards the desk together, slowly, cautiously, as if by staying as a group it would be somehow safer. Each patient's name was read aloud, and the mother gently nudged towards the anesthesiologist to whom she would surrender her baby. They arrived wordlessly and stood before us.

The mother of my young patient looked like a child herself. Eighteen, maybe nineteen at the most, and short, all four feet something of her before me, eyes cast down. She held her son close in with her arms encircling him, seeming to protect him from those around her. Perhaps she was trying to hide his face, as well. I took the infants chart in my hands, a manila folder with a single piece of paper inside. I couldn't read the writing, but a Post-it note on the outside told me all I really needed to know: "11 months, 8.2 kg. Combo." So, a really young one scheduled for a combination cleft lip and cleft palate repair. I swallowed nervously. On the top right-hand corner was his name, Jose something, the place he had come from, and then his travel information. It read, "Two days. First day canoe, second day bus." I reflected on when they made the arduous trip to the hospital the week prior, the mother had no assurance her son would even be chosen for surgery. But she did have hope, and that had been enough for her to make the long journey.

Julie took the folder from me. She spoke Jose's full name, reading from a sheet of paper that listed the operating schedule for our room. The mother looked up; our eyes met. She half-smiled, warily, hopefully. I held out my arms, and she gently, reluctantly, gave her son to me. I cradled him in my arms. He was really small for his age, light as a feather. I guessed he was only in the lowest tenth percentile of weight, maybe from malnourishment from his facial defects, maybe from poverty, maybe from both. I pulled back the blanket that covered his face and saw the unmistakable features I would come to recognize in many of my patients that week: a kind of copper sheen to his skin, dark chocolate brown eyes, straight jet-black hair, and prominent cheekbones. Jose's eyes peered up at me, seemingly curious about the Caucasian man who now held him. Below his cheekbones was a vicious curled gash in his upper lip, off to one side, which ripped all the way up to his nose. The skin was twisted and purplish, pulled tight and scarred white at the edges. It was split wide enough that you could see a gap in his pink upper gums as well, extending inside to the area where his palate was cleaved in two. He was beautiful. As Psalm 139 describes, fearfully and wonderfully made.

I held Jose gently in my arms and smiled at the mother. She looked back at me with dark eyes, wide. She reached up and put her hands on my shoulders. Quickly, she drew me in and pulled me down. She kissed me softly on my cheek, holding me there for a moment. As she withdrew, I saw her lips were quivering. A solitary tear ran down her cheek from one eye. Without a word, holding Jose close to my chest, I turned and strode to the OR.

Chapter 13

EQUALITY

EVERY MISSION TRIP I went on made me appreciate more how fortunate I was to live in the United States. We had better drugs, better hospitals, better equipment, better everything. Of course, not everyone in the U.S. had equal access to the better everything, but once they got to my OR, they did. For those without insurance or financial resources, that usually meant urgent or emergency surgery, where no patient would be denied care. Practicing in Nashville, in a tertiary hospital, I took care of many dirt-poor patients who had no ability to pay.

And also, because I worked in Nashville, I couldn't help but end up taking care of some pretty rich or pretty famous people from time to time. The first time I did so, I was working in our Pain Clinic and an elderly gentleman came in with his wife. He had a pinched nerve in his back and needed an epidural steroid injection. Standard stuff. Without looking close-ly at the chart, I introduced myself, and he greeted me, stating his name. It immediately clicked. I looked at his features. Of course. It surprised me, in a way, how he looked just like he did on TV, receiving awards for Male Entertainer of the Year and others. I stammered out something about how much I loved his music. Then I did the epidural exactly the same way I would have with any other patient.

You can't play favorites. No single patient is special in the Pain Clinic or the OR because every patient is special. Each receives the same unwavering care, whether young or old, rich or poor, famous or unknown, insured or destitute, likable or despicable. If you treat famous people differently, it just means you're doing all the other ones wrong. A doctor deviating from what he or she knows is right, trying too hard to please, is how celebrities—think of Michael Jackson—have sometimes received disastrous care. I often re-marked during my career that if you had enough fame and enough money, you could buy the worst care in America.

As a doctor, you have to be willing to have a patient dismiss you. I was once asked to do a celiac plexus block on a famous singer who suf-fered from vague abdominal pains and was habituated to a high dose of a narcotic. For that procedure, I would place two long needles deep near the spinal column to destroy a waystation for pain signals being sent to the brain. I would never do that procedure in anyone other than a terminal cancer patient because it was so effective in blocking pain signals that you could have an intra-abdominal catastrophe, such as a perforated gall blad-der, and be unaware of it until you were deathly ill. I advised her that the procedure would be inappropriate. Then I took a breath and added, "I don't like telling you this, but I think our best plan is to get a psychiatric consult and get you into rehabilitation treatment." She told me she couldn't do that because her family depended on her income. I replied that if they loved her, they would accept the temporary loss of earnings. She thanked me, and I left. The next morning, I ran into her internist. He smiled at me and said, "Well, Dave, our girl has taken you off the case." I wasn't surprised. Several years later, I heard on the news she had died from a narcotic overdose.

The same concept of equality is mandatory when taking care of a doctor or his or her spouse. You might give a little more "white glove" treatment, spending a few extra minutes with them, but the medicine you practiced never wavered. In a way, treating patients equally is an extension of the "Golden Rule," doing for others, all others, as you would have them do for you.

Dr. Klock, a retired internist, was in for emergency repair of a com-plicated hip fracture following a bicycle accident. Dr. Klock was tall, a few inches north of 6 feet, and looked younger than his nearly 70 years. He had sandy colored hair, still thick, and piercing blue eyes. He carried a trim, athletic build, so I figured he was pretty serious about his bicycling. I had met him a few years earlier, and I was certain he had no memory of me. On that occasion, I thought the best description of him was "stately." He carried himself with confidence, yet projected warmth and humility, perhaps grate-ful for the way his life had gone. He reminded me of the Hollywood actor Charlton Heston, and I could envision him riding that chariot in Ben-Hur, cracking the whip high above his head.

Shortly after finishing his residency in internal medicine, Dr. Klock had switched careers and launched one of the most successful health care-related businesses in America. He had been hugely successful—he was fabulously rich and world famous—but his leg was a mess. He had had a prior total hip replacement, and the femur—the thigh bone below the metal prosthesis—was shattered. On x-ray, you could see so many pieces that it looked as if it had exploded. In addition to replacing the hip, the orthopedic surgeon, Dr. Joe Slaughter, was going to have to sort out all the shards and somehow mend the largest ones together. It would be a long, difficult operation.

I saw Dr. Klock on the afternoon of the injury, a Saturday when I was the on-call anesthesiologist. I did a brief physical exam and then looked over his lab work. I thought about my options, but only for a moment. I could do either a general anesthetic where he was totally unconscious, or I could choose what we called a neuro-axial technique. The latter was divided into either an epidural or a spinal. Each of those would numb the lower half of his body. The difference between them is that with the epidural our local anesthetic is placed just outside the membrane that holds in the CSF ("epi" means "outside," and "dural" refers to the membrane), while the anesthetic is placed directly in the CSF for a spinal. (There are two other categories of anesthesia that may be chosen for other operations. When a surgeon uses a local anesthetic to numb up the area he or she is working on and we sedate the patient, it is called a MAC, for monitored anesthesia care. A regional anesthetic is where we use local anesthesia to bathe the nerves going to an extremity that is being operated on. For example, we might do a brachial plexus block—the brachial plexus is the group of nerves innervating the arm—administered under the collarbone for wrist surgery.)

My plan was a no-brainer. I looked down at Dr. Klock and said, "We'll get you off to sleep for this. You should do well."

He looked up from his stretcher and responded, forcefully, "I really want you to do this with an epidural. That's what I had in Chicago when they did my original hip operation." He had a tone that said he wasn't going to take "no" for an answer.

I didn't hesitate. "No, we're not going to do that. I think that's a bad choice." And since this was an emergency case, there was no time for a colleague to replace me who might satisfy his desire.

Before I had a chance to explain, Dr. Klock furrowed his brow and persisted, "Look, I did really well in Chicago with the epidural. Never felt a thing. No nausea. I really want an epidural for this."

I responded firmly, repeating, "No, we really can't do that. I believe I would be doing you a disservice if I did an epidural. As a re-do hip, and especially with the severity of the break, you might have a good bit more blood loss than usual, and the epidural would make holding your blood pressure steady more difficult. And you're going to be on your side in the OR far longer than you were in Chicago. That might be tough to tolerate at some point. If you got to where you were so uncomfortable I needed to get you off to sleep, it's a lot more difficult to do so with you on your side. You really need a general anesthetic for this."

Dr. Klock frowned. His steely blue eyes seemed to bore into me. He wasn't used to anyone not following his directives. He pled his case once more. "Look. I'm sure you can do this just as well with an epidural. They told me in Chicago I would have *less* blood loss if I had an epidural than if they put me to sleep." Dr. Klock was like many physicians when discussing anesthesia—he knew just enough to get himself into trouble.

I continued, "Well, that's sometimes true in an ordinary case. But your surgery is not going to be ordinary. That's a really nasty break you've got, and I need to balance the chance of reducing blood loss using an epidural with encountering bleeding that is far more than usual due to the magnitude of the injury, where an epidural can be less safe. The balance falls to the general. This isn't a close call. I really must insist."

He wasn't giving up. "I'm not at all happy about having a general."

I came back, quickly. "I understand. But I'm not real happy about that break. Trust me, you need the general. Sorry."

Wearing down, he continued, "Is there anything I can say that might change your mind about this?"

I shook my head. "'fraid not."

Dr. Klock relented. As with any good doctor, he knew when to give up and accept his role as the patient. He would be treated equally well as anyone else, even if he didn't want to be.

I checked his IV and saw he had come from the floor with an 18 gauge. I would have preferred a larger one, a 16, but I decided the 18 would do. I figured I could always start another in the OR if he needed it. I waded back into the chart and saw that Dr. Slaughter had asked for 2 units of blood to be set up, so it looked as if he also anticipated more bleeding than usual. Most total hips were done without the need for any transfusion.

We entered the OR, and I decided to anesthetize Dr. Klock while still on the stretcher so we could avoid a painful transfer to the operating table. As we put our monitors on, the CRNA that I was working with on call that day, Anna Gifford, noticed the IV. "Dr. Alfery," she asked, "is that big enough for this case?"

"Yeah, I think so. If Joe gets into anything significant we can always start another one."

We got Dr. Klock to sleep and then moved him to the operating table. We positioned him all the way on his side, his arms stretched out on an arm board, a pillow between them. About thirty minutes into the operation, everyone was relaxed and chatting. Joe was marveling at the complexity of the break, fiddling with the bone fragments he could get to, trying to figure out how he would reassemble the pieces. Since the leg muscles had been ripped apart by splintered ends of bone, the anatomy was pretty indistinct, the upper thigh looking like a torn end of tenderloin steak.

As Dr. Slaughter worked, I said, "Joe, he told me he was supposed to go to Geneva, Switzerland today at 3 pm. There's no way you can get to Geneva from Nashville if you leave at 3 pm."

Joe chuckled. "David, he doesn't fly on the same plane that you and I do." Of course, I thought. He'd be taking a company jet, one of several he had at his disposal.

Then, all at once, Joe shouted, "Holy shit, get Gemanch in here!" Dr. Rudy Gemanch was the vascular surgeon on call that day. He was aware of the operation and was upstairs making rounds, having told Dr. Slaughter he would be available if needed.

A fountain of blood shot out towards the wall and ceiling, squirting two or three feet into the air with each heartbeat. Dr. Slaughter had somehow torn the femoral artery, the large vessel that runs through the groin and down into the leg. Almost immediately, he yelled, "Damn it, I can't get a hold of this thing! I can't get it!" The vessel had retracted into the wound, and its opening was obscured by broken bone, tissue, and blood.

An uncontrolled bleed from a femoral artery can cause death in less than 5 minutes. And within the first minute, Dr. Klock had lost well over a unit of blood, maybe two. I shouted to the circulating nurse, "Call Randall. Tell him to come to the OR immediately!" Dr. Arthur Randall was my back up doctor on call. I figured he was at home and his arrival could take up to twenty minutes, but I was preparing for the worst.

I opened up the 18 gauge IV all the way and saw a pitiful, slow dribble of intravenous fluid. I mentally cursed myself for not starting an additional IV when Anna had questioned it. Why had I insisted on the general anesthetic while not demanding a larger IV? I had gotten a little sloppy, breaking my rule that if you thought you *might* need an additional IV, that meant you put it in from the start, even if that turned out to be needless.

Anna grabbed a bag of a fluid called hetastarch, a product that would substitute for a blood transfusion until we could get his units into the room. She slipped it into a pressure bag and inflated it to force the fluid in quickly. The dribble turned into a thin stream, still far slower than what we needed. I yelled to the circulating nurse, "I need his 2 units from the blood bank, along with four more type specific. And they should be working on cross matching four more." At least for now, I had learned my lesson and was preparing for a massive transfusion, whether we needed it or not.

Joe cursed and yelled to his assistant, "Pull the retractor over here . . . No, that's not it! Here!" And then, "Get me exposure! Suction, damn it to hell!"

During all this struggle, with each beat of the heart, Dr. Klock's femoral artery squirted blood from the field, occasionally up into the air like a fountain, but more so into the cotton cloth Dr. Slaughter held against it, trying to physically close the tear by pressing down until Dr. Gemanch arrived. Despite the pressure, a deep lake of blood filled the wound. Joe let up a couple of times to try to find the opening in the artery, but he gave up quickly each time. On the last attempt, the height of the squirting was far lower than it had been, but only because the blood pressure had dipped dangerously low.

Joe's chest and abdomen were drenched in blood, with a steady flow dripping off his surgical gown and pooling in puddles of sticky red liquid on the floor. Some blood had squirted onto his facemask and forehead, but there was no time to wipe it off. Within minutes, Dr. Klock had lost 20 per cent of his blood volume. Then 30.

The circulating nurse sprinted out the door. Almost immediately— though it felt like forever—she returned with an Igloo ice cooler containing six units. While we waited, I slapped a tourniquet on Dr. Klock's arm to start a second IV, silently cursing myself again. I noticed a rare trembling in my hands. I think it reflected both the gravity of the situation and the added pressure one feels when caring for a VIP. There is simply no upside. You are expected to provide perfect care for those individuals, and you do so in anonymity. No one in the public ever knows your name, and even the patient likely won't remember it for long. But if you fall short and the patient doesn't do well, the whole world might wind up knowing who you are. I briefly pictured the front page of USA Today with a story about how Dr. Klock had died in the Operating Room during surgery while under the care of an incompetent anesthesiologist. And at that point, Dr. Klock was well on his way to doing just that.

The second IV, a 16 gauge, went in right when the blood showed up, so Anna and I hung two units simultaneously. We put them both on pressure bags, but Dr. Klock was still bleeding far faster than we were replacing it. The beeping of the pulse oximeter monitor had picked up speed, because the falling blood pressure had caused his heart rate to reflexively speed up. We had put our automatic blood pressure cuff on the STAT mode, and that meant that it immediately recycled every time it had completed a measurement. The pressure, while initially stable, had been falling with each measurement, and I had tried to keep it up by giving increasingly large doses of a drug to constrict his vessels. But those doses were becoming less effective.

I looked at the automated cuff monitor for blood pressure and it read "Error." Often, when a blood pressure has fallen to a dangerous level, the machine cannot measure it accurately and resorts to "Error." With the STAT mode in operation, I heard the soft whine of the cuff being pumped up again. I watched as it slowly deflated, with progressively lower numbers flashing—98, 92, 85, 80, 72, then Error again. Shit, I thought. I felt down for a pulse and found I it barely perceptible. No wonder it wouldn't record. I switched to a more powerful blood pressure drug and gave a large dose. I also dialed back the amount of anesthesia Dr. Klock was receiving.

Then I moved to insert a central line in his neck. That would be a two-port IV that went deep into the jugular vein, and placement would not be an easy task with our patient lying on his side. Thankfully, I had placed thousands in my career as a cardiac anesthesiologist, and it slid in without difficulty. With the dual lumens, we now had four IVs! The circulating nurse cried out, "Gemanch is on the way!" Then added, "Randall's coming!" The blood pressure monitor finally produced a reading in the 70s, right at the edge of circulatory collapse, even with the additional doses of vasopressors.

And then, as suddenly as the bleeding had started, it stopped.

Joe yelled, "Got it!"

We had transfused two full units of blood, had a third partly in, with Anna in the process of hanging the fourth. The crisis had lasted less than ten minutes. I breathed a sigh of relief and began a quick mental debriefing. The first thing I thought was, damn, I should have had that second IV in place. That mistake could have cost him his life! And then, thank God I insisted on the general.

A few minutes later, Dr. Gemanch arrived, breathless as he stormed into the room. Joe gave him a brief report, and he went to the sink to wash his hands. He would do a repair of the femoral artery, but no longer as an emergency.

Dr. Randall crashed through the OR door a few minutes later. By then the fourth unit of blood had been fully transfused, and we had started a fifth. The blood pressure had stabilized. I raised my hands in front of me as if to say, "Stop. Sorry." I apologized for the distress call that, in retrospect, was not needed. Arthur stayed for a few minutes of casual conversation and glanced down at our anesthesia record. The vital signs showed a jagged line, with some highs and lots of lows. Several drops of blood had spattered and smeared on it, as well. He looked closer, and he must have seen the name stamped on it. He looked up at me, surprised, then at the patient, and then back at me. He exclaimed, "Holy smoke! This is Dr. Klock?"

I nodded.

Dr. Klock's care hadn't been perfect, but at least it was equal to what any other patient would have received.

Chapter 14

ALLEGIANCE

MOST DOCTORS WHO HAVE to take call will tell you it's the worst part of their job. Those are the hours when most non-medical people don't have to work—the nights, the weekends, the holidays. You miss a lot of ordinary life. Whatever they're calling you for is either urgent or a true emergency; otherwise, it would wait until the next day. Also, those are often the times when the sickest patients present themselves, and you're usually all alone to take care of them. If the emergency happens in the dead of night, you may be dead tired as well. Of course, no matter how inconvenient the time or circumstances, whenever you're summoned to care for a patient, you owe them your full effort.

Whenever I was on call, even after having practiced medicine for many years, it was nerve wracking. Even if things remained quiet, there was always that underlying anticipation of what I might have to deal with and anxiety about whether I'd be able to manage it properly. When on over-night duty, invariably I had trouble getting to sleep—my mental edge would simply not let me relax and drift off. Once I was asleep, if my pager jarred me awake, it was as though I had been hit by a cattle prod, with a screeching noise I swore could wake the dead.

One night, my pager went off at around 11 pm, after I had been asleep less than thirty minutes. I snapped awake, then called the Nursing Supervisor, Harry Rogers, whose number had appeared on the pager screen. He apologized as if he had done something wrong to call me. "I'm sorry, Dr. Alfery. Dr. Holland has a patient in the ICU who needs to go to the OR. The team is on the way in."

That was bad. I figured a little more than an hour to get the patient down into the OR, then a minimum of an hour and a half, likely more, for surgery, then a half hour to get the poor soul back upstairs, and then a half hour to get back home. So, at the least, I could count on three or four hours out of bed. Also, with the patient coming from the Unit and thus critically ill, it meant I would have to be sharply alert in order to concentrate all my mental capacities. Sometimes, when you got called in for a brief ICU procedure, such as putting a central line in a patient, you could kind of sleep-walk your way through it, then get back to sleep with less difficulty. Not with this. Plus, the call occurred before we had CRNAs taking call with us at night, so I would be doing the case alone.

I groaned as I crawled out of bed and yanked on my clothes. On the way out, I stopped in the kitchen and poured 2 cups of instant coffee into a thermos container. I tried to gauge my caffeine intake when called in the middle of the night, trying to balance what I might need to stay alert with the thought that if I got lucky, I might find myself trying to get back to sleep a few hours before dawn. But it took more than coffee to get mentally geared up for a difficult case in the wee hours. You had to will yourself to be alert, just set your mind that you would be totally attentive, like slapping your consciousness across the face to get sharp. I really don't know how doctors do that, year after year in practice, but somehow, we all do. I guess that's the idea behind working so much at night during our training—to make it ingrained.

There was little traffic on the road, so I drove fast and made good time. It was always a scramble to get everything prepared when I took a patient from the ICU to the OR in the middle of the night, so getting there a little early was key. I had the coffee finished by the time I pulled into the hospital parking lot.

My first stop was the OR. We kept a room prepared for emergencies, so all I needed to do was check out my anesthesia machine and draw up some medications. I hustled to the main elevator bank and the door opened quickly. There wasn't much traffic, this being the "graveyard shift," with fewer staff working than during the day. When I got to the floor of the ICU, I hurried down to C pod, and as I got there a ward clerk pointed me to the correct room.

The patient was alone in the room, except for his nurse who was trying to arrange the spaghetti-like jumble of clear plastic tubing running into him into some kind of order for transport to the OR. "Hi," she greeted me, as I entered. "So, you're the lucky one."

"Hi," I mumbled back. I stopped to look at the patient. He had a breathing tube and was hooked up to a ventilator, which gave off a squawking alarm every few breaths. The airway pressure it delivered exceeded the upper limits it was set for. Rather than breathing in synchrony with the machine, the patient tried to inhale while the machine was still exhaling, and vise versa. We called that "fighting" the ventilator, and it usually meant a patient wasn't getting enough oxygen.

The patient, who looked to be in his 80s, maybe even upper 80s, appeared to be sleeping, but I knew that most patients looked that way when they were critically ill. No sedation was required, as if all their energy and consciousness was taken up just fighting their illness. His hair was mostly white, and thin, wispy, but also greasy and uncombed. He hadn't been shaved for a couple of days, and his chin had a slick sheen to it, either from sweat or from saliva that dripped from the edge of his mouth. Beyond the hospital gown his arms were bare, and I could see areas of hemorrhage under his skin where IV attempts had failed, leaving little splotches of red-blackish stains. Band-aides had been taped over some of those areas, as if they might hide the insertion failures, but the discoloration had spread well beyond their edges.

Maybe it was his big boned frame, but something about the patient made me think he had been a pretty tough guy in the past. There was nothing tough about him now. He looked defenseless. The lights in the ICU cast everything in a kind of bright but artificial pallor, and maybe that contributed to making him look cold, almost lifeless. I don't think you can smell death, but you can recognize the odor of the dying, and I thought he had it—a kind of sickly, old and decaying smell, like last week's dinner left too long on the counter. His blood pressure on the monitor was hovering in the high 70s, dangerously low, and his heart rate was fast, around 135. Whether he knew it or not, he would be dead within hours if something weren't done.

I got the history from the nurse. He'd been admitted from a long-term care facility a day earlier, with no immediate family available. There was only a niece or something like that back East. He had fairly advanced Alzheimer's, so he couldn't give any history, only moan in discomfort when he was moved to his bed. Over the next 24 hours, while the ICU doctors—also called intensivists—had tried to figure out what was going on, he had gotten progressively sicker, to the point where the breathing tube had to be placed. Also, he had begun to produce acid in his bloodstream. Acidosis, as it was called, was a sinister sign, and it often meant that something was dead inside. In this case, the intensivists were concerned that he had "dead bowel," meaning he had suffered a sudden cessation of blood to his small or large intestines, or both. The general surgeon on call, Dr. Samuel Holland, had been contacted to take him to the OR to confirm the diagnosis and try to repair whatever was wrong.

There were a number of ways the operation could go. First, it might be a negative laparotomy. That would mean Dr. Holland would find everything normal inside, and he would simply sew him back up and return him to the ICU with the cause of the acidosis still unknown. The second scenario would be that there was a segment of bowel that was deprived of blood for long enough that it required removal. Cutting out that dead bowel would entail a resection that might last anywhere from an hour to several hours, but it would give the patient a chance of recovery. Or perhaps there was an occlusion of a blood vessel to a segment of intestine that could be relieved, also giving the bowel a possibility to recover. The last scenario was that all the intestines would be infarcted and dead. In that case, like the negative laparotomy scenario, Dr. Holland would simply close the abdomen and return the patient to the ICU. Death would follow within hours.

As I considered the possibilities, I wondered why we would be operating at all. Had that niece back East said to go ahead? Did the intensivists push for surgery, just reflexively trying to fix whatever was wrong in a patient? Even in this patient? With that Alzheimer's at an advanced state, I thought, there are worse ways to go than simply not operating. But it wasn't my call.

I don't know why I felt so tired that night. Maybe it had been a particularly hard and long day. Maybe because I had only a few minutes of sleep when awakened, and I knew that much of the night would be spent in the hospital. Maybe because I knew this would be a tough case with the patient so sick. Regardless, I had to draw on my reserves and resolve to do the job the best I could. I would have to work hard in the OR to get the blood pressure and pulse stabilized and to correct his metabolic imbalances, let alone put him under general anesthesia safely. I decided no matter the outcome, some special preparation was mandatory. I let out a weary sigh, knowing that would take an extra 20 or 30 minutes, depriving me of that much more sleep time whenever I might get back home.

We got the patient down to OR 10, our room for after-hour emergency cases, and transferred him to the operating table. I attached his ECG and blood pressure cuff and hooked him up to the anesthesia ventilator. He no longer was bucking and breathing against it. That lack of effort was an even more ominous sign that he was running on empty, physically overwhelmed and giving up. The blood pressure had fallen to the 60s on the trip to the OR—a critical level—so I quickly gave a medication to boost it up while I prepared to insert the required catheters. The pressure rose into the 70s but wouldn't budge above that with additional injections. Not good.

With the blood pressure so low, the first thing I needed was an arterial line in order to see a beat-by-beat readout of the level on my monitor. I could barely feel a pulse—necessary in order to place the arterial line—as I fumbled through several failed attempts. I cursed repeatedly, quietly at first, but then louder with each miss. After leaving several puncture marks and some bleeding under the skin on the left wrist, I moved over to try on the right side. To my surprise, the pulse felt stronger there. Damn it, I thought. If I had slowed down enough in the first place, I would have examined both wrists for pulses before my attempt and chosen the better side to begin with. But it was so fucking late, and I was so fucking tired. I was just trying to save time, just trying to move fast, and I had grabbed the wrist that was most readily available. Thankfully, I got the arterial catheter in on the right side with the first attempt.

I hated to add additional time, but I also needed a central line, a large double-lumen IV in the jugular vein in the neck, where I could get medications rapidly into his circulation. The OR team waited patiently while I prepped the neck and inserted it. The patient never even flinched, another worrisome indication of how gravely ill he was.

I gave some bicarbonate to help correct his acidosis and started an epinephrine infusion, and within a couple minutes the pressure rose to nearly a hundred, a response far better than I had thought possible. Finally, I turned on an anesthetic agent. Not much, but likely enough to make him amnestic in the event he lived through his hospitalization.

The OR team stripped him bare and prepped his abdomen. It was grotesquely distended, looking like he was seven or eight months pregnant. The swelling was likely from food and liquids not moving through his intestines normally, and also from gas building up inside that would stretch out the bowel. The circulating nurse painted his abdomen with a brown antiseptic and stepped back to allow Dr. Holland to place the surgical drapes.

Lying naked on the table with his arms outstretched at ninety degrees on arm boards, it looked as if a bizarre crucifixion was taking place. The only thing that assured us he was still alive was the rapid beeping of his blood oxygen level from my monitor.

As Dr. Holland placed the drapes and called for the scalpel, I found myself thinking—maybe it will all be dead. And not just thinking it, but kind of wishing it, as well. I reasoned that it wouldn't be the worst thing for him, maybe even better. This guy has had a good long life, and every life must come to an end. He's got Alzheimer's and no family, at least none that live anywhere near him. Can't have much of a life with Alzheimer's and no family.

Looking back, I want to believe that my only reason for thinking that way was a matter of patient benefit. If he had inoperable dead bowel, we would simply close him up and his suffering would be over in a matter of hours. But I know also mixed in there was my thinking—God, I can't remember when I've been this tired. I'm so fucking tired my head is spinning. I just want to get back to bed and somehow get through this night and start over tomorrow.

Don't get me wrong—my allegiance was to the patient, if he had any chance at being saved. I would do whatever was required to give him the best possible care. If that meant we would be in the OR half the night, or even all night, there would be no slacking off if there were any chance of saving him. But still, the nagging thought—wouldn't it be easier for everyone if that kind of care was not indicated and we could just get this over with?

I knew allegiance to principles was an essential component of living and that fidelity to those I cared for was the glue that cemented my doctor-patient relationships. Life without loyalty was both empty and meaningless. Further, part of my responsibility as a human being was to try to make the world a little better place each day. I didn't know if my desire to end the case quickly fulfilled that duty, but I didn't think it would make the world any worse, either.

At 12:30 am we began surgery. Dr. Holland pushed the knife deep into the skin just below the belly button—the medical term is umbilicus—and pulled it down to the pubis below. The skin parted quickly and peeled back, as if it were the outer layer of an onion. The glistening fat that opened up underneath would normally be bright yellow and have areas that briskly bled a vivid red. Instead, the fat looked almost grey, and the few areas that did bleed had dark, almost black blood slowly oozing from them, another ominous sign. The bleeding sites were attended to by quick jabs of the Bovie as its heated tip coagulated vessels, causing the surrounding fat to bubble and burn with a pop and sizzle as if someone were cooking bacon on a skillet. Thin tendrils of smoke floated upwards from where the heat had been applied, weaving gently under the bright OR lights as they rose towards the ceiling. Smoke signals—danger ahead.

Dr. Holland got into the abdomen pretty quickly, and we knew right away that things were bad. The bowel, coated with slimy greenish-brown stool, was distended, so it immediately pushed itself out of the incision like a balloon being blown up from inside the belly. The distention was clearly caused by gas forming on the inside of the wall where the intestine had died. The segment that had pushed its way out was purplish black, a sure sign of bowel death. With feces free in the abdominal cavity, there must have been a place in the intestines that had been deprived of blood flow long enough that it had ruptured. There is a smell that emanates from perforated dead bowel that you never forget, a smell so powerful and offensive it kind of knocks your head back so that you instinctively breathe through your mouth. It is the aroma of feces that have spilled into the abdomen and been allowed to fester, along with the infected and decaying tissue around it. That smell was present, thick, overpowering, covering us like a dense fog, enveloping every crack and crevice of the OR. The circulating nurse scampered to a cabinet to get out a bottle of wintergreen concentrated scent. She opened it and put a dab on our OR masks right under our nostrils, so when we inhaled, it's sickly-sweet odor might cover the smell of death.

Dr. Holland stated simply, "Well, that's no good," and he extended his incision up above the umbilicus the full length of the abdomen. He pulled out the swollen bowel, all of it, loop by loop, and laid it onto the now flat abdomen. The intestines looked like sausage gone bad, dark and glistening, bulging and rotten. Most important, all of it looked dead. All that remained was for Dr. Holland to feel for arterial pulsations in the mesentery, the sheet of tissue within which the blood vessels traveled. If there were a pulse, there would be a remote chance he could remove a blood clot beyond it and restore blood flow to the gut, though that would require the bowel to be able to recover from what appeared to be a fatal cessation of blood flow. I found myself again thinking, and in a way wishing—no pulse. I wondered if Sam was thinking the same thing.

After a couple of minutes, Dr. Holland said, "It's all dead. Let's close." Quick. Final. A death sentence. The patient would be sewn up and brought back to the ICU, and that niece back East somewhere would be called and told, "We're sorry, there was nothing we could do." The epinephrine would be stopped, other supportive measures not administered, and death would arrive quickly. But I would wait until we got to the ICU to stop the blood pressure support the epinephrine was providing. Ironically, for a patient who was destined to die within hours, we would do everything possible to avoid his expiring while still in the OR. Statistics were kept on OR deaths, and hospital ratings could suffer.

Right after Dr. Holland spoke, the circulating nurse said something like, "Oh no, that's terrible." It was as if she were pulling for the patient, the way maybe I should have been. Suddenly, I felt ashamed. I wondered if there was something wrong with me. Should I have been rooting for a curable process in this 80-something year old Alzheimer's patient with no family to care for him? I had to admit, I hadn't been. There was a large part of me that was thankful there was nothing more to be done. In fact, once the terminal judgment had been made, I felt something like a second wind, a little burst of energy and wakefulness needed to finish the case. A bit of euphoria, even. I kept my mouth shut and did my job as Dr. Holland began closing the abdomen. I tried not to think.

Less than an hour later, I delivered the patient back to the ICU. There was the arterial line and a central venous line in place that would no longer be needed, but since they were there, we hooked them up. They would just allow the nurse to monitor and record in more minute detail the patient's inexorable exit from this life. The last thing I did was make sure there was plenty of narcotic and sedative on board to make certain that, even if the patient somehow rallied for a few hours, he would not suffer.

I drove home fast. I tried to let myself relax and prepare for sleep, but I was still pretty amped up when I pulled into my garage at nearly 3 am. It would always take a period of time to unwind enough to sleep after a case like that—you can't just turn a switch and shut off your mind. I quietly slipped back into bed, careful not to awaken Joyce. I was bone tired, yet it seemed to take forever to drift off.

For some reason, I still reflect back on that case from time to time. I've come to terms with my thinking that night, or at least as close as I can. I tell myself that what is important are actions, not thoughts. We can't control our thoughts any more than we can our dreams, can we? We can manage what we do, though, and I swear I would have given that man everything I had if he had been salvageable. I would have rallied and fought the good fight for him with all my might and delivered him back to the ICU with the absolute best chance of living through his hospitalization had Dr. Holland found something he could fix. But he didn't. In the end, I didn't decide his fate. Those intestines died all on their own. Still, on the nights when I remember those events, just as it was on the night they happened, it's not easy to fall asleep.

Chapter 15

GRIEF

SOME ANESTHESIOLOGISTS ARE FORTUNATE never to be faced with a death while caring for a patient, but they are generally those working in low-risk settings such as outpatient centers or plastic surgery suites. If you worked in so-called tertiary hospitals as I did, the ones where patients were sent who were too sick to be cared for in community hospitals, you invariably had patients under your care who perished.

For much of my career, an anesthesiologist headed up the code team. Each day, one of us answered when the "code beeper" went off, dropping whatever we were doing to hurry to the crisis somewhere in the hospital, then command the resuscitation of a patient whose heart or breathing had stopped. We directed the code until either the patient was successfully resuscitated, we gave up and pronounced the patient dead, or the patient's regular doctor arrived to assume care.

When the code ended in death before the patient's personal physician got there, it fell to us to discuss the outcome with a grief-stricken family. These were the worst possible situations, where a doctor totally unknown to a family has to deliver the worst possible news. I never received instruction during medical school or anesthesia training on how to talk to a patient's family after their loved one had died. I think we were just expected to pick up the art of giving comfort along the way. I was fortunate to have Dr. John Carter as a mentor while I was a surgery intern, so I had an excellent model to follow.

Whenever a patient died, we would assemble in the quiet room, usually with several nurses to lend support. I had a few rules that I followed: I started with a physical connection, some kind of touch to a family member after the introduction. I looked in their eyes, went slowly, and kept it simple. I was asking them to assimilate the most devastating news they might ever hear. The conversations were invariably disquieting, but once you met the family, there wasn't much else to say other than that your efforts at saving their loved one had failed. Reactions ranged from sad resignation to uncontrolled wailing. As a total stranger, it was hard to offer the nurturing they needed. Part of me always felt I had failed the families, not because the patient had died, but because I feared I hadn't said enough or chosen the best way to say it.

The first death I experienced in the OR, the baby with the congenital heart disease, hit me really hard. And during my years of training, any death was hugely disturbing. But when I went into private practice, I developed a kind of emotional armor. An OR or ICU demise was just the dirty downside of my work, something unpleasant that happened from time to time. For many years, I was pretty successful at shielding my emotions, but as I got into the later part of my career, deaths started affecting me more. Maybe the way they should have all along. After a couple of decades in practice, maybe they hit a little closer to home. As the poet John Donne famously said, "Each man's death diminishes me, for I am involved in mankind. Therefore, send not to know for whom the bell tolls; it tolls for thee."

For deaths in the OR, the fatality was most often either related to the surgery or to the overall sickness of the patient. Few of these deaths came as a total surprise, occurring as they did in very high-risk settings. When a patient died on the operating table, there was an unwritten rule that the surgeon would trudge off for a solitary visit with the family while everyone else busied himself or herself with cleaning up the mess left behind. There were instruments to collect, floors to mop, sponges to count, paperwork to be filled out. The IVs would remain in place, as would the breathing tube, sticking out of the mouth like some huge plastic straw, for the pathologist to document during the postmortem examination. Sometimes, as we began our work, the patient still lay naked on the operating table like a lifeless mannequin, as if somehow forgotten, bruised and bloodied. It wasn't that anyone was uncaring or intentionally disrespectful. But the impact of an intra-operative death, even if almost anticipated, still left most of the OR team jarred, off kilter. Within a few minutes, though, one of the nurses would dutifully notice the oversight and cover the body, as if to hide the visible evidence of our collective failure.

No matter the age of the patient nor the circumstances of the death, everyone who participated in the care had a stark reminder that their days were numbered, that one day it would be one of them whose life had come to an end. For some, denial could generally brush off that reality, while older caregivers felt more the impending inevitability of their eventual passing. The fortunate ones used these events to reflect on their own lives and how they might make them more meaningful.

I would watch the surgeon leave the room, solemn and quiet, and wonder, intellectually, how difficult the conversation was going to be. But over time, I sympathized with the surgeons more and more, imagining how they must feel. Only in a case where a patient suffered a death due to an anesthesia mishap or complication would the anesthesiologist be the bearer of bad news, and I was thankful I never faced that situation.

About twenty years into private practice, I stumbled onto the idea that it might be comforting for the surgeon if I went along to share the burden of speaking with the family. The first time I made the offer to a surgical colleague, he was startled, but he said, "I've never had the anesthesiologist come with me before. I would love to have you along." Other subsequent surgeons reacted in much the same way. With my first trip, it was obvious my joining the conversation was beneficial for the family as well as to the surgeon, that I too could offer meaningful words of comfort. To my surprise, I found it was comforting for me, as well. Sharing with individuals the intensity and pain of the loss somehow lessened the grief we all felt.

Looking back, I'm astounded it took me so long to adopt this protocol. After all, we all know how comforting it is to an individual's relatives when we attend a visitation or funeral, even if we knew the person who passed away only casually. Somehow, the weight of loss is made a little lighter by sharing the burden.

About ten years before I retired, I had a patient named Billy who had suffered serious heart abnormalities at birth that had required surgery during his infancy and childhood. The procedures were palliative and not curative, in that they did not correct the original structural problems, which were too simply too severe to allow total repair. These temporary fixes to the plumbing of the heart allowed Billy to live, but with a reduced activity level and shortened life expectancy. He had experienced a reasonably happy life up until to the time we met, but over the prior several months his condition had gone rapidly downhill. More shortness of breath, more discomfort. Another operation was required if he was to live much longer.

By that time, however, his heart was so weakened from its structural abnormalities and the surgical options for improvement were so limited that the cardiac surgeon, Dr. Donald Dickson, had quoted a 40 to 50% chance of mortality. That was a stunningly high risk for any operation, a figure almost unheard of. It presented a devil's choice for the patient and his family: face a significant chance of death in the OR with the hope of perhaps several more years of life, or an agonizingly slow death over the next few months. They opted for Dr. Dickson to do his best.

I met Billy's mother and father during a pre-operative visit in the boy's hospital room on the afternoon before surgery. I remember his parents well, though I have long forgotten the specifics of his cardiac abnormalities. They seemed quietly at peace with the decision to proceed. I mentioned to them that the entire team was expert in what we would be doing, with everyone specifically trained in cardiac work, and that Dr. Dickson was the best, having training in both adult and pediatric heart surgery. They already knew that. With a decades-long relationship, they had seen their surgeon grow from a young, well-respected cardiac specialist in an academic center to the senior surgeon at a prestigious tertiary hospital. They had put their trust in him with the prior operations, and they would again. As with most cases where there was a high surgical risk, I didn't see any need to amplify it, so I said simply that I would give the best care I could. The parents politely thanked me.

I turned to Billy and wondered briefly what his parents must be feeling. Everyone wants a little more time: time to watch a child go through school, time to watch him reach adulthood, time to see what he becomes. There is never enough time.

Billy sat quietly, smiling. He was a friendly young man with some mental disabilities, as is often the case when an infant is born with significant heart abnormalities. He sat through my brief physical examination and discussion saying very little, just an occasional "Yes, sir," or "No, sir." I'm not sure if he fully understood what he was in store for or how high the risks were, or that there were any risks at all, for that matter. He had been a wonderful and obedient son, always trusting his parents, and he would continue to do so. I said my goodbyes and left the room thinking how, in some ways, Billy was a lucky young man. Other than for the condition of his heart.

That evening, I went home and hardly said a word to Joyce. "What's wrong?" she asked.

"Just a big case tomorrow. Just thinking." There were times I needed to talk to her and times I needed to be alone. She quietly left the room.

I couldn't get the mortality figure out of my head. "There is a 50:50 chance this young man will die tomorrow" kept repeating in my mind, like a carousel wheel slowly turning around, again and again. I knew everything my cardiac CRNA and I did would have to be performed perfectly for Billy to have the best chance of surviving his surgery. I went over in my mind what special drugs we would need to help get Billy through. I recalled what I had often joked to my partners about anesthesia: "When you do a case, there are 50 ways to screw it up. If you think of 25 of them, you're a genius. And you ain't no genius." The expression seemed a lot less humorous that evening.

I thought about the case when I went to bed and until I drifted off to sleep. That obsessive worry about what lay ahead with a particularly high-risk surgery the next day plagued me my entire career. The higher the risk, the more I ruminated. I awakened several times in the middle of the night, each time with the case in my mind. When my alarm jerked me awake at 5:20 am, I arose exhausted, and I immediately thought of Billy.

When I entered the OR at 6:35 am, I greeted the surgical team with, "Hi kids. How's everyone?" The response was muted. Each person was preparing his or her work area in silence, on edge. My CRNA, Lela Hanson, had been in the OR for about twenty minutes when I arrived. Somehow, I felt more confident about the anesthetic when I saw her. Considering her the best cardiac CRNA in our practice, I had specifically assigned her to help with the case. Doing so was the highest compliment I could give for her abilities, but it would come with six or seven hours of punishing high wire work.

"Good morning," I said, trying to sound upbeat. "Thanks for being here. This one's going to be tough."

She didn't hesitate. "Wouldn't miss it," she said. We briefly discussed what we should do with the case. As I expected, she had anticipated all the drugs I thought we would need, and she had them drawn up and ready to administer.

I went out to the holding area and started an IV in Billy's hand. He seemed cheery, seemingly unfazed by the sting from the local anesthetic I placed in the skin. I gave him a small dose of Versed to make him calm for the trip into the OR, though I wondered if he even needed it. When we brought him into the room, he was only mildly sedated, and he looked around at the equipment and personnel with what appeared to be more curiosity than apprehension. Having been no more than a few years old at the time of his two childhood surgeries, likely, he had no recall of the misery involved. As he wiggled himself over to the operating table from the stretcher, he smiled. He was happy. He trusted us. He bravely allowed us to place invasive intravenous and arterial catheters without flinching, and with a look of equanimity.

One of the monitors we placed was a Swan-Ganz catheter, so named for the two cardiologists who had invented it. It allowed us to measure pressures in his heart, and the initial readings showed his pulmonary artery pressure, the pressure in the vessel that went from his right ventricle to his lungs, was dangerously high. It was so high, in fact, that had this been a normal case, we would have cancelled the operation. But this was no normal case. We simply had to accept his pulmonary arterial pressure as part of what made the mortality risk so high.

Billy drifted off to sleep as Dr. Dickson came into the room. He seemed unconcerned, though I suspect his impassive look reflected more resigned acceptance than denial of the dangers that lay ahead. No one spoke of the difficulty of the case, perhaps for fear of somehow jinxing it. I slid the transesophageal probe into place and Billy's heart image appeared on the monitor screen.

Dr. Dickson asked, "Can we look at the right side, Dave?" I twisted the probe clockwise to visualize Billy's right ventricle, and we saw it was dilated, contracting poorly against the high pressure we'd just recorded. The tricuspid valve (so named for its three leaflets that opened in unison) leading into it was also leaking badly, with much of the blood going backwards into the right atrium when it contracted. "Well, not unexpected," Dr. Dickson murmured. He went out to the sink alone to wash his hands.

After prepping and draping the chest, Dr. Dickson made his incision around the old vertical scar, cutting it carefully on each side and then discarding the skin off the table. I wondered, was he confident enough to already be thinking about the cosmetics of the closure? When he opened the chest cavity and freed the scar tissue from around the heart and great vessels, another residue from earlier procedures, the anatomy didn't look like anything I had ever seen before. I recognized one artificial conduit for blood Dr. Dickson had placed during Billy's first years of life, and it was bulging from pressure within it. Expanding each time the heart contracted, it looked as if it might burst.

After we went on bypass, Dr. Dickson cooled and arrested the heart, and he then set to work. Whatever he did would be a strictly jerry-rigged palliative procedure, making the best of the options available. Occasionally, Dr. Dickson let out an audible sigh, as if to relieve the build-up of anxiety, and as he worked, he shook his head back and forth repeatedly. He didn't like what he saw. But he worked steadily, patiently. Near the end, he spent a long time asking for additional suture to tidy up leaks where blood vessels had been sewn. It was critical to have things go as smoothly as possible once Billy was separated from the bypass machine and his heart was beating on its own.

Lela started several infusions of vasoactive agents while the repairs were being finished. These drugs would make the heart work as efficiently as possible once it took over from bypass. I hooked up the pacemaker cables that Dr. Dickson had passed over the ether screen and turned on the current. Looking down, I could see the upper chamber, the right atrium, moving inward as it beat, and then just a moment later the lower chamber, the right ventricle, slightly squeezed. The fact that the electrical impulse traveled normally through the heart was encouraging. I thought, maybe this won't be so bad. But then I looked at the muscle. Since we were still on bypass, the heart was empty of blood while it contracted. In that setting, where it did not have to push any blood out to the lungs, it should have looked vigorous. Instead, the ventricle barely moved. It lay there, kind of twitching inwards, almost limp. Billy's heart was slowly dying.

There was no way Billy would ever get off bypass without the assistance of an intra-aortic balloon pump. While it was being inserted, we maximized the doses of the drugs we were giving to make the heart pump more strongly, and we also adjusted the doses of the other agents that would reduce the resistance it would work against. The room was almost completely quiet, with only the hum of the bypass pump and the beep of my ECG calling out. Occasionally, we added the sounds of Dr. Dickson requesting an instrument or suture or the muffled voices of Lela and I discussing the drugs we were giving.

We came off bypass slowly. As the right ventricle struggled to eject blood against the pressure of the pulmonary artery, it increased in size with each contraction. Blood returning from the body filled it more and more with each cardiac cycle, but the ventricle was unable to empty itself. We could see it growing larger with each chirp of the oximeter, blowing up the way a child might blow up a balloon with a series of small breaths. Within ten or twelve beats, the ventricle was stretched and swollen, and it barely moved inwards at all as it contracted.

"Back on," Dr. Dickson commanded. He breathed in and out, slowly, audibly, voicing a long sigh. He picked at the areas of his repair, prodding here and there, as if he might find something that was causing the right ventricle to fail. Everything was intact, everything fixed to the extent it could be. He let out a few "tsk, tsk" sounds as he surveyed the carnage. We waited another fifteen minutes while he attended to a minor bleeding site, as if pretending that this would solve the problems of a heart that could no longer pump forcefully enough to sustain life.

We tried coming off again. This time there was little discernable movement of the right ventricle at all. "Back on," Dr. Dickson again commanded, this time after only a few beats of the heart.

We waited some more.

There was little talk in the OR, but there was constant communication and understanding, though, as we all looked at each other and made our own individual physical gestures. One might shake her head back and forth, another look up at the ceiling, another arch his eyebrows, another sigh. Each of these spoke the same sentence: "Billy is going to die."

Dr. Dickson looked across the screen and asked, "Well, Dave?"

I shrugged my shoulders. "Don, we've got him maxed on epi, norepi, milrinone and vasopressin. We've even given some methylene blue. I'm not sure we have any more tricks to pull out."

Of course, Dr. Dickson knew all that. I said it just to reassure him.

We tried again to separate from the heart-lung machine, and this time the right ventricle ceased contracting at all. It bulged up from the chest cavity, stretched out like a glistening purplish sac. It looked like it was ready to explode. The only assurance we had that it was still alive came from the heart's electrical activity—the pacing rhythm was displayed in a beautiful white trace crawling across the deep blue background of the monitor screen.

"Back on, back on," came the order.

But we knew we were done.

After another ten minutes we tried one final time, knowing it was hopeless, just going the extra mile. The deterioration had been startlingly quick, a cardiac collapse that announced Billy had given everything he had during his life, and he had no more left for the OR.

Dr. Dickson asked, again, "Well, Dave, what do you think?" Shouldering responsibility for giving up was a crushing burden for him to take on alone, and as a colleague and close friend, he was looking for validation.

I answered softly, "We did everything we could. There are no more arrows in the quiver. You've given him his best chance."

Dr. Dickson responded with a slow movement of his head, back and forth. Then, in a firm voice, he announced to the room, "That's all."

He stepped back from the OR table and slowly ripped off his gloves and gown, then his mask. That in itself announced that our efforts were over. He looked sorrowful, his face drawn and empty. He had taken care of this young man from the very first surgery in infancy, and then another one when Billy was a young boy. The family had been with him for over two decades and had sought him out specifically for this last procedure, even though he was now late in his career. Their long journey together was over.

As is generally the case with a death in the OR, the room was silent as Dr. Dickson stepped back. I reached over and turned off the anesthesia ventilator. The cardiopulmonary pump tech turned off the heart lung machine. There was still electrical activity of the heart appearing on the monitors, but once I turned off the pacemaker it ceased after only a couple of futile attempts on its own, the last spark of life extinguished. Billy died within seconds. I murmured to Lela that I would be leaving, going with Dr. Dickson to see the family. She grasped my upper arm and gave it a brief squeeze. I leaned back and whispered, "You're the best."

Dr. Dickson and I left the room together. Right outside the OR we encountered the death stretcher, already placed there for transporting Billy's body to the hospital morgue. Death stretchers are gurneys constructed in a manner that hides a body being transported, sparing live patients from seeing the shrouded form of a fellow patient who has died.

We walked slowly, as if we were dragging our feet out of mud with each step, perhaps unconsciously trying to delay the discussion that was to come. As we lumbered to the ICU, we talked quietly about what had happened, how it was apparent just how terribly sick he had been even before we put him to sleep, how difficult the anatomy had been to work with, how the surgical options had been so limited. And how painful and discouraging our work could sometimes be. A famous French surgeon, Rene Leriche, once said, "Every surgeon caries within himself a small cemetery, where from time to time he goes to pray."[1] Presumably, they visit the tombstones

1. Source unknown.

of patients such as Billy. I don't know how often a surgeon might wander back to his or her own graveyard, but I suspect it is no more than is necessary to remind themselves of the fragility of the lives they work to sustain. Dr. Dickson had added a fresh headstone.

We arrived at the quiet room with the family and ICU nurse already there. Billy's parents were prepared, as much as a father and mother can ready themselves to hear that their child has died. They had understood the risks the surgery entailed going in, and they had been regularly updated with the difficulties we had faced coming off bypass. Still, their grief was palpable, their faces reflecting anguish as they sat close together, waiting only to hear confirmation.

Dr. Dickson pursed his lips and grimaced as he sat close to them, his head tilted forward. Maybe it's just the way I felt, but he seemed to have aged since the operation had started almost six hours earlier. His eyes were moist. He licked his lips, pursed them together, and took a breath. He paused for a moment as he held it. Then he began, in a voice that was soft, weary, almost inaudible, whispering, "I'm so sorry. I'm so very sorry."

The parents looked at each other, gave a little gasp, and gripped their hands together. Then they shook them up and down, fast, as if holding on to something that was trying to slip away. Maybe it was Billy. No matter how prepared you think you are to hear that kind of news, it's still like a dagger in the heart when it comes.

Dr. Dickson continued, seeming to gain strength. Both parents nodded affirmatively, understanding, moving from sorrow to resignation as they began to accept that this chapter of their lives was completed. Their trust in Dr. Dickson had begun 26 years earlier and continued to that moment, a connection that was tangible and profound. It was the kind of doctor-patient bond that an anesthesiologist could never have with a family, because our encounters, though often intense, are rarely built on shared history. Dr. Dickson spoke a good bit about the difficult journey of their son's health, about what they had all been through, and repeated how sorry he was that it had come to this end. Then he said, "I think you know Dr. Alfery, the anesthesiologist," and sat back.

Before speaking, I thought, with all the changes I had seen in medicine over my career, they don't make them like Dr. Dickson, anymore.

Billy's parents looked at me intently, leaning forward. Like Dr. Dickson, I began by saying how sorry I was for their loss. Then, I said, "I want you to know it was a privilege to care for your son," just as I had witnessed

Dr. John Carter say to the parents of our 19-year-old burn patient Grace so many years before. They nodded in unison. I then assured them their son had been totally asleep for the entire procedure, that there was no chance there was any consciousness, any awareness, any suffering. They nodded again.

I finished by telling the parents something I had observed on almost all occasions with a death in the OR. In that setting, death does not come easily. In fact, whether in the OR, in the ICU, or with a sudden cardiac arrest on the floor, death never seems to come easily. There is truth in the old expression that one does not easily give up the ghost. Cardiac function eventually stops, but it does so in a gradual, fitful, downhill slide, with a progressively weaker and weaker heartbeat, until there is only electrical activity but no pumping function at all. And then, finally, the flat line you've seen so often on TV.

So, the final thing I said was, "He was a real fighter. He fought really hard all the way to the end. He must have had a really big heart to fight that hard." The parents leaned into my words, their eyes glistening. They shook their heads in unison again. I went on to describe how, no matter how damaged Billy's heart was, no matter how significant the non-repairable abnormalities were, no matter how demanding were the stresses the operation had put on it, his heart had done its best to continue to beat. For Billy, much of the fight had occurred in the last few years of his life, but he had fought right until the end, just the same. For that, he must surely have been blessed with a special heart, one of strength and determination. He had fought hard. We had all fought hard. In the end, it was simply not enough.

This very tough business out of the way, we were able to talk about Billy and his life. A little ray of sunshine peeking out from the clouds, it seemed, to lessen our grief. The parents spoke of how Billy had always had it tough, but he had met his challenges as a fighter would. How he faced each surgery the way he faced life, with courage and equanimity, always trusting his parents, always trusting his doctors and nurses, and always fighting. For Billy, with mental challenges added to his cardiac ailments, options in life were limited, but that didn't stop him from trying to live it to the fullest. Our short discussion finished with a small celebration of how much Billy the person, not the patient, had lived.

At the end, we all stood. Billy's parents embraced Dr. Dickson. They held him close, seeming to not want to let go. Maybe releasing him would sever a final link to Billy. At last, they separated. They stood together, their heads held high. They looked at peace.

We left the room and turned towards the Operating Room. As we walked together, we looked ahead and hardly said a word.

EPILOGUE

WE ARE ALL GOING TO DIE. Some will die young, while others will last so long that they simply wear out in the end. In my medical practice, I witnessed both extremes, as well as most everything in between. But as Charles Franklin famously wrote, "No one gets out of this life alive." Death is the one thing that all people have in common. It is also the one thing that we share in equally; there is no favor shown to the rich, the powerful, the clever, the famous, the devout, the profane.

One day early in my practice, I saw a dirt-poor farmer succumb from a heart attack, and then later that same day, a legendary singer who had been named Entertainer of the Year by one of the country music societies pass away following emergency cardiac surgery. The farmer might have been thrilled to meet the singer in life, and after he died maybe he did in the afterlife.

Another time, a few days before his death, a multiple Grammy Award winner needing a celiac plexus block for cancer pain asked if I would deliver some signed records to the patient I had scheduled before him. The purpose of the gift was to get the other patient to allow the singer to go first. I gently declined and told him we didn't manage our schedules that way, that I would get to him just as soon as the first patient was finished. While money and fame meant just about everything to some individuals while they were alive, it meant almost nothing as their life ended.

We spend almost all of our youth blissfully unaware that our end will come. When someone we know who is very old dies, we accept it. They had a good life, and their time had come. But when a previously healthy young person is taken suddenly, unforeseen, it is a slap in the face, a painful reminder that our days are numbered. In fact, since the day of our birth, every day brings us one day closer to death. So, whether young or old, every day is a gift. I can't tell you at what age a single day is most appreciated, though when asked, many will say its greatest value is right at the age they are presently living. Sadly, it is seldom thought of until old age arrives. Now that I am reaching that point in life, I can assure you, you try to make up for lost time when you get there.

Most people, regardless of age, need to be reminded of their own mortality over and over in order to appreciate their ever-approaching end. Even the awful image of a dying Gypsy boy or the memory of a moan brought by the passing of a middle-aged mother of two following a routine cosmetic procedure were mostly swept aside from me by the trivialities of daily living.

For many, regardless of age, the thought of death is a frightening intrusion on their consciousness. Our discomfort is lightened by euphemisms that avoid the stark reality of dying. If you were approaching death, you were said to be circling the drain or cashing in your chips. Once dead, someone would have bought the farm, bit the dust, or gone belly up. Others might use softer phrases such as passed away or taken a last bow. More bluntly, the Grim Reaper makes his appearance, and we end up dead as a doornail. Despite my Christian faith, if I find myself lying awake in bed late at night, in the dark and unable to sleep, the thought of death—and especially ruminating on an exit filled with discomfort—sometimes brings a quickening of my own heartbeat.

Some deaths come quickly, unexpectedly. But for most, there is a time when one can anticipate that the sun is setting over the horizon, and, for better or worse, prepare for it. Susan Sontag wrote:

> Everyone who is born holds dual citizenship, in the kingdom of the well and in the kingdom of the sick. Although we prefer to use only the good passport, sooner or later each of us is obliged, at least for a spell, to identify ourselves as citizens of that other place.[1]

I handled more passports than I care to remember during my time working in medicine. As patients grew sicker, I witnessed their travel become more and more restricted, more and more difficult, more and more uncomfortable. By the end, for many their journey was limited to excursions only from a hospital or ICU room to an Operating Room. Some never made the trip back.

Many wish to die a "good death," where the passage out of life is gentle, where loose ends are neatly tied up, accounts are settled, old grievances forgiven, and goodbyes spoken. Not many do. For most, there is a gradual

1. From the introduction to Susan Sontag, *Illness as a Metaphor and AIDs and Its Metaphors*. New York: Farrar, Straus, and Giroux, 2013.

and frustrating loss of control over just about everything that allows us to function. And for many, there is pain. For some, life is uselessly prolonged with ineffective treatments in a desperate attempt to hang on just a little longer. The fight is made all the tougher because it is a battle we know we will ultimately lose. Even so, whether by the insistence of the patient, the family, or the doctors providing their care, I witnessed over and over the inability to accept that death at the end was normal, simply dictated by Nature, just as life was at the beginning. Fortunate people, though they die a solitary death, do not travel with their sickness to their destination alone. Ideally, friends, competent caretakers, and most of all, family, accompany them.

Someone once said old age, disease, and mortality are the price we pay for being human.

In my career, I crossed paths with death, or at least the possibility of death, far more often than I wished. And many more times, I cared for patients who were grievously ill. That taught me quite a few lessons, though I profess to be no more an authority on the subject of death than I am on how to live.

Early on, I was flippant and callous. During my first ten or fifteen years of practice, I felt invincible, immortal. When I intersected with death, it hardly occurred to me that I would one day suffer my own. It was like a distant continent, one that I couldn't picture myself ever sailing to. But as I matured and felt my own mortality, I gave death, and those who faced the possibility of death, the respect it deserved. Over time, I know my interactions with patients who were facing their passing made me a better doctor. I hope they made me a better person.

A wise man once said that we live two lives. The second one begins when we realize that we only have one.

In this book, I have tried to impart some of the things that I learned along the way of eight years of medical school and training and then a thirty-six-year career as a cardiothoracic anesthesiologist. I saw how thin the line could be between life and death that patients walked, where a series of seemingly minor events could line up perfectly and cause a demise, like the layers of Swiss cheese allowing the knife to fall through the holes unhindered. Or how a single unexpected and unnoticed catastrophic mistake could kill you. In that regard, medicine is not much different than our ordinary lives, where we never know until it's too late that the car coming towards us on the 2-lane highway will suddenly veer into our lane. Life is fragile, the journey perilous, the path uncertain.

Practicing anesthesia all those years was a humbling experience, both knowing I could often have done far better, but also having the honor of treating patients at a critical time in their lives. Like almost all doctors, I found nothing more rewarding than a patient entrusting me with their care. It took me having a family member facing death to really understand that I was no different than any non-medical person in that situation, that we are all at the mercy of our medical professionals and our illness. My faith helped me realize the limitations of what I could do, and I came to believe in a power much greater than I possessed. Though faith by no means provided me all the answers about life, it has allowed me to be content with asking fewer questions. As the years passed, I understood the gifts I received from relationships dwarfed any material possessions. I learned to express my emotions to those I loved far more as an older person than when I was young.

I was continually amazed by the patients I was privileged to take care of. From their complete trust in my abilities to the grace they showed while facing death, they exhibited the best a physician could ask for in the doctor-patient relationship. I learned how sharing loss with others could somehow lessen grief. I saw the suffering that a family experiences when a condition spins wildly out of control, and it taught me the need to care for them as well as the patient. I came to view my patients, as the Oath of Maimonides advises, as fellow creatures in pain. When I was able to alleviate physical pain, there was nothing more rewarding. Most of all, I saw the importance of the human connection, expressed more than 2,000 years ago by Philo of Alexandria, a Hellenistic Jewish philosopher who wrote, "Be kind, because everyone you meet is fighting a great battle."

As most any old person will tell you when looking back on a career, my years in medicine passed far faster than I ever thought possible. While the nights on call seemed to drag on forever, the years flew by. Blink, you're thirty. Blink, you're forty. Blink, you're fifty. Blink, you're sixty. Blink, and your eyes never open again.

Through my work, I have been honored to enter the rooms of many dying patients. When I was involved with their care, my toils seemed to me a blessed obligation. The rooms of those approaching death were almost always quiet places, sometimes almost sacred. Most often, only the closest family members were present. There was no talk of diplomas awarded, honors achieved, contracts signed, gold records sold, or money made. In the end, what mattered most was the people the patient loved and who loved them.

As I traveled through the decades, my priorities changed profoundly. Now, as I near the end of my race, I run with more urgency, knowing I am ever closer to the finish line. Every day is precious. The big question is, how should we live each and every one of them?

Sadly, we often don't have much of a say in our death—the time, the circumstances, and sometimes even in our comfort level. But we do have choices in what we do until we reach that point. I can't tell you that I have found all the keys to knowing how to live, to finding the balance between all the competing forces that influence our daily lives. I do know that it is imperative to constantly try to find it, though. To paraphrase the 20th Century poet Heartsill Wilson, "What you do today is important, because you are exchanging a day of your life for it." That's a high price we pay for that day. Our challenge is to live it as if our life depended on it.

ACKNKOWLEGEMENTS

I CONSIDER *Saving Grace: What Patients Teach Their Doctors About Life, Death, and the Balance in Between* as a fifty-year project. The first eight were spent learning medicine and anesthesiology, the next thirty-six taking care of patients, and the final six writing the book.

Over this time period, the patients I was privileged to care for were the one indispensable element. I owe my career to the individuals who put their trust in me, a total stranger to most, day after day, year after year. None of *Saving Grace* would be possible without them, nor would most of the life I have lived. My greatest wish is that I have done justice to the patients I was honored to care for.

In 1976, I was admitted to LSU Medical School in New Orleans by the skin of my teeth, and ever since, I have been enormously thankful. I could not have received a better medical education than at LSU or been schooled in the presence of nicer people—fellow students, house officers, and teachers. I am equally thankful for LSU educating my middle daughter, Janna, thirty years later. Geaux Tigers!

During my surgical internship, Kenneth Holwitt, Rick Bell, Steve Hubbard, Ward Griffen, and Ballard Wright served as physician role models and mentors. These humble men—giants in my mind—likely have no idea what a positive influence they had on my life. Chief influencers during my anesthesia training were Lou Marsh, who guided my path, and Jon Benumof, who allowed me to spend my year of specialty training under him. Other key physicians who mentored me during my years in San Diego included Larry Saidman, who always insisted I have a reason for what I was doing, Connie Ward, Bill Nelson, Brian Donahue, and many more. Barry Zamost accompanied me in my training like a brother.

In private practice, almost all of the surgeons I worked with were friends as well as colleagues. Most held me to a standard that brought my care to the highest level it could be. Early on, William Edwards Sr. and I fought many a battle, but always for the good of our patients. I wish I had been mature enough to acknowledge what a great man he was. The cardiac surgeons I worked closest with for decades, who also elevated my care, were Phil Brown, Larry Pass, and Davis Drinkwater. All were unique and exceptional in their own ways. Karl Van Devender, who is something of a physician Renaissance Man, was a source of inspiration over my practice life, and I am grateful for the advice and encouragement in writing given to me by Karl and by his wife, Ann Patchett. Two other non-physicians who offered encouragement and guidance were literary agent Frank Breeden and Gerry House, the latter a dear friend and the funniest man I know. Influential surgeons over the years include Joe Mulherin, Tim Schoettle, Everette Howell, Verne Allen, Vaughn Allen, Mark Cooper, Joe Chenger, Mike Santi, Bob Roberts, Seenu Reddy, Dean Knoll, Bill Polk, Lucien Davis, Jack Fisher, Patrick Maxwell, Richard Gere, and so many more. I admire all these individuals. I hope I have done justice to the surgeons I describe in *Saving Grace* and who I was so fortunate to work with.

I learned early on to surround myself with exceptional partners. There are countless anesthesiologists who worked by my side in the anesthesia groups I was a part of who, by their keen intellect, skilled hands, or work ethic, elevated my care. The most important, and the doctor I always aspired to be, was Robert MacMillan. Others include Lee Ferrell, Mike Stabile, Patrick Forrest, Brad Worthington, Julia Sawyers, Art Runyon-Hass, Steve Santi, Calvin Burrichter, Allen Buck, Duncan Nelson, Jack Price, Ken Sears, Dyer Rodes, Bob Riedel, Jane Thomas, Tom Thomas, Leon Ensalada, Kenny Williard, Thom Adkins, Marc Siegel, Chris East, Chris Watke, Kathyrn Killman, Steve Sperring, Paul Seitz, Tom Toomey, Mike Hays, John Dalton, and the list goes on. All the anesthesiologists who worked with me in Anesthesia Consultants of Nashville as well as those at Centennial Medical Center and Williamson County Medical Center made me a better doctor. Non-U.S. physicians who taught me that the best and brightest are by no means confined to America were Marcus Oziel, Xavier Marquez, Luis Gaitini, Michael Frass, Felice Agro, and Tibi Ezri. The doctors who inspired me and whose friendships sustained me at the American Board of Anesthesiology were John Ammon, Steve Slogoff, Carl Hug, and Dick Stypula. I still can't believe they welcomed me into their group. Ozan Akca, Brian Ball, and Peter Szmuck show how important your medical friends are even when they live hundreds of miles away.

As I mention in the book, I worked with CRNAs during all my years in practice. As a group, these were amazingly dedicated and skilled individuals, though many stand out especially—Leilani Herbert, David Beasley, Kale Streetman, Brad Rickett, Gracie Gerlock, Sue McSwinney, Mark Pepper, Randa Pesz, Roxanne Lenz, Debra Dement, Mathew Johnson, Amanda Orrand, Trevor Eldred, Mary Constantine, Lori Horner, Amanda Parsons, Randi Binkley, Aaron Elmore, Shaun Collins, Jonathan Grooms, Jackie Dodson, Charles Knapper, Jenny Riordan, and I could name dozens more. Know that I regarded all of you as colleagues more than as employees, and I benefitted from working with each of you. So often you made me look good because you did your job so well. As I always said, "You're the best."

On my road to becoming a Christian, there were many guides and counselors. My friend of over fifty years Peter Gilbert was sent to me, twice, to be influenced by his own conversion. Of the many physicians who influenced me, Mike Kaminski (to his great surprise, I suspect), served as a catalyst simply by an overheard comment he made in the doctors' lounge at Parkview Hospital more than thirty years ago. Then Buzz Martin kick started my journey in Nashville, John Leonard showed me it was safe, Joe Thompson encouraged me as a gentle mentor, Sam deMent served as an example, and Pastor Earl Gibbs held the safety net as I jumped over the chasm from nonbelief to belief. Pastor Jim Thomas has led our church family at The Village Chapel for almost twenty years and is the one from whom I shamelessly stole the term Cosmic Concierge. Also, the simple "I got baptized" is pure Andrew Klavan, all the way.

"*Ungawa*" was lifted from the brilliant Wall Street Journal columnist Dan Neil.

Though I didn't mention it in *Saving Grace*, I was blessed to have made several medical inventions during my career. Writing the book, to my surprise, was a far harder endeavor, and it would not have been possible without a number of key individuals helping me along the way. Dan Lazar of Writer's House was the first literary agent who believed I had talent, and he worked faithfully with me for a year. Dan, thank you for believing in me and encouraging me to go on, even though we did not cross the finish line together. While working with Dan, Jane Rosenman edited my original manuscript, showing me how much I still had to learn about writing. Carolyn Savarese, my agent at Kneerim and Williams Literary Agency, did cross the finish line with me, and completing the project would not have happened without her. Carolyn, thank you for keeping reading after the first two sentences, as I challenged you to, but most of all for believing in me. Not to mention your tireless efforts in working to find a publisher. Nina Ryan is a wonderful editor who suggested many of the transitions from one chapter to another and added other important improvements. I have to give a special shout out to William Patrick, writer and editor extraordinaire, who offered countless refinements of the writing. No one can polish a manuscript the way you can!

What busy best-selling author would ever take the time to read a manuscript by an aspiring new writer and then offer their professional opinions to be quoted by the publisher in marketing the book? Well, for me there were four: Dr. Paul Ruggieri (*Confessions of a Surgeon* and *The Cost of Cutting*), Dr. Henry Marsh (*Do No Harm* and *Admissions*), Dr. Arthur Kleinman (*The Soul of Care* among many others) and PhD and RN Theresa Brown (*Critical Care*, *The Shift*, and *Healing*). Not only are each of these individuals beautiful writers, they are also kind and generous. I am humbled and grateful to each of you for taking the time to read Saving Grace and then offer me encouragement.

I am excited to work with Wipf and Stock to publish *Saving Grace*. Mathew Wimer, managing editor, thank you for believing in the book. And thanks to all the individuals at Wiph and Stock for the type setting, proofing, marketing strategy, and all the other unseen elements that go into putting a book into press.

Saving Grace would not have been written without the support of my family. The cover photo was envisioned by my brilliant artist nephew Andrew Witt, who also optimized its presentation. My thanks to my youngest daughter Kim for lending me her hand to place underneath mine. I have two sons-in-law, Dr. David Larson and Travis Tingey, who are vastly different in their interests but who share equally in their devotion to my daughters Janna and Kim, who they married. I lean on both as I would a son. Finally, with all I was privileged to do in my training and career, I ended up doing far more of it than I wished. As a physician in a "service" medical specialty, one that does not have their own patients but services other doctors' needs (in my case, obviously, when they needed an anesthesiologist), the time I spent in the hospital was dictated by how busy our operating rooms were. Nashville grew enormously while I was in practice, and our hospitals did as well. It seemed my anesthesia group was always short of doctors and CRNAs, always behind in trying to hire more. As a consequence, Joyce carried the burden of running our household and doing most of the child-rearing. To my daughters Alli, Janna, and Kim, I wish I could turn back the clock, and I am only thankful your mother did such a wonderful job with each of you. Joyce, we always said it takes two. There would have been no *Saving Grace* for me without you.

CPSIA information can be obtained
at www.ICGtesting.com
Printed in the USA
LVHW081524080323
741196LV00028B/286